Praise for *Catholic Matters*

"A new book from Fr. Richard John Neuhaus is always cause for celebration, and *Catholic Matters*: *Confusion, Controversy, and the Splendor of Truth* doesn't disappoint. He is not just a fine theologian but a thoroughly engaging writer, with an eye for the charming anecdote . . . To read Neuhaus is both to meet old friends and to be continually surprised."

—*The National Review*

"Neuhaus's new book . . . gives us a detailed and up-to-date account of the kind of Catholicism . . . which he aims to inject into the heart of American public life."   —*The New Republic*

"This finely written book offers a refreshing analysis of an emerging Catholic identity in the United States. It does not skirt the contemporary scandals that embroil bishops and local congregations but adroitly transforms these thorny issues with liberating words of truth. With the mind of a theologian and the heart of a pastor, Neuhaus authors a clear commentary on American Catholic self-understanding in the early 21st century. . . . [*Catholic Matters*] is realistic, courageous, and hopeful as it describes a new generation of faithful Catholics reawakened by clerics like Popes John Paul II and Benedict XVI."

—*Library Journal*

"Richard John Neuhaus is the most underrated writer in America. . . . Neuhaus writes with the kind of graceful prose that one associates with Hemingway or the essays of Aldous

Huxley or Lionel Trilling. Yes, the man is first and foremost—according to him anyway—a priest. But as his terrific new book, *Catholic Matters*, shows, Neuhaus knows how to put pen to paper. Whether Catholic or not, it's the kind of book one reads in one gulp, buoyed by tight, graceful sentences that one thought became extinct with the death of Orwell or Chesterton."

—*The American Spectator*

"There is a lot of meat in this relatively brief book, but Neuhaus's careful service of it makes it as palatable as it is rich."

—*Booklist*

"Readers acquainted with Neuhaus's previous books and his work with the magazine *First Things* will be most interested in this latest tome on the state of the Catholic Church . . . Neuhaus devotees and others interested in the issues he raises will find here a thoughtful exposition of Catholicism's present moment."   —*Publishers Weekly*

"This is the story of how one priest discovered the way of grace and glory that is being Catholic. Writing with eloquence, deep intelligence and wit, Father Neuhaus guides us past all the confusion and controversy and lets the splendor of truth shine through. If you're a serious Catholic, if you want to be a serious Catholic, if you want to know what it means to be a serious Catholic, read this book."

—Peggy Noonan, author of *John Paul the Great*

Catholic Matters

Also by Richard John Neuhaus

Catholic Matters

Confusion, Controversy, and the Splendor of Truth

Richard John Neuhaus

BASIC
BOOKS

A Member of the Perseus Books Group
New York

Hardcover published in 2006 by Basic Books,
A Member of the Perseus Books Group
Paperback published in 2007 by Basic Books

Library of Congress Cataloging-in-Publication Data

Neuhaus, Richard John.
  Catholic matters : confusion, controversy, and the splendor of
truth / Richard John Neuhaus.
    p. cm.
  ISBN-13: 978-0-465-04935-6; ISBN-10: 0-465-04935-4 (hardcover)
1. Catholic Church. I. Title.

  BX946.N48 2006
  282.09'0511—dc22

                                                    2005034569

ISBN-13: 978-0-465-04936-3; ISBN-10: 0-465-04936-2 (paperback)

10 9 8 7 6 5 4 3 2 1

Avery Cardinal Dulles

friend and mentor

Contents

1 | The Church We Mean When We Say "Church"

During those never-to-be-forgotten days of April 2005, I kept a "Rome Diary." The significance of what happened there and then weaves in and out of all the reflections that follow. I flew into Rome's Fiumicino Airport two days after the death of John Paul the Great, accompanied by an ABC network filmmaker who was making a documentary and had been following me about for several days. She had arranged for a car and dropped me off at the Hotel Michelangelo, adjacent to St. Peter's, where I would be staying for a little more than two weeks. Later that day I wrote the first installment of the Rome Diary:

> Thousands upon thousands, an endless flow of humanity down the long nave of St. Peter's. They have come to see him for the last time. For all the crowds, the place is strangely quiet. A Roman friend with connections got me into the space reserved for dignitaries. There, on the catafalque only a few feet away, was what remained.

Kneeling at the prie-dieu, I had only a few minutes, certainly no more than ten, to think what I wanted to think and pray what I wanted to pray in this moment I had so long anticipated and so irrationally hoped would never come. Odd thoughts came to mind. His back was straight again, after all those years of being so pitiably hunched and trembling from the Parkinson's disease. He seemed much smaller. Perhaps not much could have been done by those who had prepared the body. He was emaciated, beaten, and bruised. The purple spots on the hands revealed the efforts, toward the very end, to find one more vein for the intravenous feeding tube. Lying there before the altar, under Bernini's massive baldachino, his head was tilted just slightly toward the right. Looking north, I thought—toward Poland.

He has fought the good fight, he has kept the faith. Well done, good and faithful servant. These and other passages came unbidden. Through my tears, I tried to see again the years of his vitality, his charm, his challenge, his triumphs; the historic moments when I admired him from a distance; and the personal encounters when I was surprised by the gift of an older brother who was the Holy Father.

I envisioned him again on October 22, 1978, in his first homily as pope, admonishing and encouraging humanity to be not afraid. I saw him in Central Park, hand on cheek in a Jack Benny gesture, mischievously complimenting the crowd's appreciation of his singing a Polish Christmas song. "And you don't even know Polish," he said. I mentioned this when I had dinner with him months later and had to explain who Jack Benny was. In such conversations we discussed Nietzsche and Schopenhauer and the ideas that had shaped and misshaped the century, and whether the end of history was at hand. (He thought not.)

Kneeling there, I smiled through my tears. Then the time came to leave. Cardinals, bishops, heads of state, and others were waiting their turn. And all the thoughts I wanted to think and all the prayers I wanted to pray were distilled in a half-sobbed, half-whispered, "Thank you, Holy Father."

Walking out of the basilica into the sunlight, a shaken friend said, "That wasn't him, he isn't there." No, I said, he is there. These are the remains, what is left behind of a life such as we are not likely to see again, awaiting with all of us the resurrection of the dead, the final vindication of the hope that his life, and his death, so powerfully proclaimed.

I will return to the Rome Diary in due course. But now we step back to see that very Catholic moment in Rome within the context of the Church in America, a context marked by confusion, controversy, and the splendor of truth. It is also a context in which being Catholic is more and more viewed as a choice, perhaps a personal preference, and not as something that really matters, and maybe matters ultimately.

Americans are notorious church-hoppers. Methodist, Lutheran, Episcopalian, Baptist, Presbyterian—it doesn't seem to make much difference to millions of American Christians. Some would say there is nothing "notorious" about that at all. Don't we pride ourselves on being a free-market society in which consumer choice is king? Why shouldn't there be a free market also in religion—or, as it is said today, in "spiritual preferences"? Church-hopping is simply church-shopping in search of a "spirituality that meets my needs." There was a time not long ago when denominational identity was much more than a matter of individual preference: "I come from a long line of Presbyterians," one heard it said. (Or Lutherans, or Episcopalians, or Baptists, or whatever.) Back then, it was not unusual for people to tell you why their church was right and others were wrong about issues such as infant baptism, or the Real Presence of Christ in the Lord's Supper, or about God's predestination of the saved and the damned.

That time is passing, if it has not already passed. Talk about right and wrong or true and false is out. Talk about what "meets my needs" is in. With the admittedly partial, although still notable, exception of people who are becoming Catholic. Switch from Presbyterian to Methodist, or start attending the evangelical "megachurch" in the neighboring exurb, and you will raise few eyebrows. People who move from one denomination to another, or from the denominational to the "nondenominational" (which is one of the biggest denominations), are exercising preferences that are, so to speak, all in the religious family. Announce that you're taking instruction to become a Catholic, however, and it is likely to prompt sharp questions. Not necessarily hostile questions, mind you, but questions of intense curiosity. Why would you want to join "them"? Catholics in America have always been the religious and, to a significant extent, cultural "other." In our exploring of why this should be, it may be helpful to take a short side road to get a better view of the religious and cultural landscape in which, to so many Americans, Catholics still seem so very, well, so very different. As we shall see, the side road leads back to our title subject soon enough.

Researchers who study denominational "adhesion power" say that the mainline Protestant churches are hemorrhaging members for many reasons. The mainline churches—for instance, United Methodist, Presbyterian (USA), United Church of Christ, Disciples of Christ, Episcopal, and now the Evangelical Lutheran Church in America (ELCA)—are today often called the oldline churches. Less kindly, they are called the "sideline churches." They once constituted the Protestant Establishment that, up to the 1950s, seemed to dominate American religion and culture so securely. Their precipitous decline in numbers and influence is often attributed to the sharp left turn their leaderships took on moral and political issues back in the 1960s. That is no doubt part of the story. Another part is the challenge posed by the resurgence of evangelical Protestants in recent decades.

Evangelicalism has a long and fascinating history. Put briefly, in the nineteenth century almost all Protestants in the United States called themselves evangelicals. Then, beginning in the 1910s and culminating in the 1920s, there was the great battle between "modernists" and "fundamentalists." Those who came to be called fundamentalists were reacting to what they perceived to be the growing theological liberalism in the oldline churches. Against the liberals, they insisted on five "fundamentals" of Christian faith: the God-inspired inerrancy of the Bible; the virgin birth and deity of Christ; the doctrine that he died on the cross in our place (substitutionary atonement); the bodily resurrection of Jesus; and his second coming to judge the living and the dead. Such beliefs were hardly novel in Christian thought. Although formulated in different ways, they were held by Christians going back to the apostolic era of the first and early second centuries. The influence of eighteenth-century Enlightenment thought, however, had by the early twentieth century led many theologians and church leaders to conclude that such beliefs were not compatible with the "modern mind" and had to be abandoned or substantively modified.

Today, people think of fundamentalism as a Southern and rustic affair (when, that is, the term is not being misleadingly applied to Muslim terrorists and others who are "dangerously fervent" about religion). In fact, fundamentalism began with a series of monographs called "The Fundamentals" written between 1910 and 1915 by distinguished scholars at major universities in Germany, Scotland, and England. Their concern was the erosion of Christian doctrine by certain forms of "biblical criticism." Sir Robert Anderson, author of *Christ and Criticism* and a Knight Commander of the Bath (KCB) does not fit the popular idea of a fundamentalist. Nonetheless, in the 1920s, H. L. Mencken and others derided fundamentalists as "yokels," "rustic ignoramuses," and "anthropoid rabble," among other choice epithets, and that is the stereotype that stuck. Thus the battle between "modernists" and "fundamentalists." The fundamentalists fought fiercely for the control of the oldline churches, and they lost.

The consequences reached far beyond the churches. Today, we hear much about the "culture war" being waged in American society. That conflict has many of its roots in the modernist-fundamentalist clash of the 1920s. Stereotypes of fundamentalism were indelibly imprinted upon the American mind by the Scopes trial, often called "the monkey trial," of 1925 in Dayton,

Tennessee. The stereotypes were imprinted not so much by the trial itself but by the brilliantly caustic reporting of the trial by H. L. Mencken and by the 1955 Broadway play, later made into a popular movie, *Inherit the Wind*. The play has been produced thousands of times by colleges and high schools, and most Americans are familiar with the picture of the sweating, bumbling, Bible-thumping William Jennings Bryan, a former secretary of state and four-time presidential candidate, vainly trying to defend the book of Genesis against Charles Darwin's theory of evolution. Opposing Bryan is the brilliantly enlightened Clarence Darrow, who makes mincemeat of Bryan's primitive dogmatism. Not at all incidentally, *Inherit the Wind* was first staged against the background of "McCarthyism," that is, Senator Joe McCarthy's reckless campaign against Communists and their sympathizers. Thus, for half a century, fundamentalism has been inseparably associated with McCarthyism and related outbursts of bigotry, intolerance, and abysmal ignorance.

As many scholars have pointed out, *Inherit the Wind* and similar portrayals of the modernist-fundamentalist controversy are more propaganda than history.[1] But there is no doubt that the fundamentalists lost in their challenge to the leadership of the oldline churches. As the story is sometimes told, they slunk away from Dayton, Tennessee, defeated, demoralized, and resigned to perpetual isolation in the backwoods of American culture, never to be heard of again. In fact, millions of Americans, forced to choose between Bryan's unvarnished religion and Darrow's highly varnished agnosticism (if not atheism), had no doubt that they were on Bryan's side. While those who controlled the commanding heights of culture were not looking, fundamentalists spent decades rebuilding their morale and institutions until, toward the end of World War II, they were confident enough to reappear in public, now calling themselves not fundamentalists but "neo-evangelicals." In fairly short order, the "neo" was dropped and America was faced with the maddeningly diverse and rapidly growing network of churches, "parachurch" movements, and entrepreneurial spiritual empires called evangelical Protestantism or, with increasing frequency, just evangelicalism. Many of them prefer to be identified simply as "Christian."[2]

Among academic students of religion, trying to answer the question of who is and who is not an evangelical is a cottage industry. All agree on at least three defining characteristics: Evangelicals have a strong view of the inspiration and authority of Scripture, a specifiable experience of being born again, and a commitment to reaching those who do not know Jesus Christ as their "personal Lord and Savior." By these measures, about a third of Americans are evangelicals. Admittedly, the counting gets a bit tricky because many in the oldline denominations, and even many Catholics, pass that three-fold test. Nonetheless, it is fair to say that Christianity in America is divided into three roughly equal parts: evangelical, mainline/oldline, and Catholic. There are a few million Eastern Orthodox Christians, and evangelicalism itself is composed of fairly distinct parts, such as pentecostalism, holiness churches, anabaptist, and Calvinist (usually called "Reformed"), but the three-part picture of evangelical, oldline, and Catholic will serve our purposes. (I leave aside for the moment whether the 5 million Mormons in America should be counted, as they adamantly insist they should be, as part of the Christian community.)

Although some depict the oldline churches as spiraling into the sideline and, beyond the sideline, into oblivion, we should not forget that millions of Americans attend spiritually vibrant local churches that are associated with oldline denominations. To the extent that the oldline churches such as the Presbyterian or Methodist or Episcopal get into the news, it is usually because their national leaderships are ordaining homosexual bishops, or calling for divestment from Israel, or advocating reparations for African Americans, or promoting something else that seems pretty odd to most Americans. But at the local level—at First Methodist or St. Andrew's Presbyterian around the corner—one frequently finds vibrant Christian communities blithely indifferent to the politicized excitements of national leadership. They go about their business doing what Christians do; they pray, praise, preach, study the Bible, baptize, observe the Lord's Supper, and try to love their neighbors. The institutional decline of the mainline/oldline, which is indeed impressive in scope and rapidity, should not blind us to the vitality of Christian faith and life in innumerable local churches. Yet the truth is that the "adhesion power" of oldline denominations is withering to the point of disappearance. The Presbyterian tradition, never mind distinctively Presbyterian convictions, has not been transmitted to successor generations and seems not to matter to Presbyterians when they move into a new suburb and join a friendly Lutheran church. What is true of the Presbyterians is true of almost all oldline denominations.[3]

With Catholics, the situation is different. "Once a Catholic, always a Catholic" it is said, and for the most part that is true. Yes, there are a lot of lapsed Catholics, but that doesn't get in the way of their insisting that they are Catholics.

There is something in the Catholic ethos that is very accommodating of human frailties. Having Ulster Protestants in mind, G. K. Chesterton observed that a Protestant typically says he is a good Protestant whereas a Catholic typically says he is a bad Catholic. But also a good many call themselves former Catholics or ex-Catholics, and thousands of them can be found in the evangelical megachurches throughout the country. For the most part, however, whether or not they've attended Mass for years or believe what the Church teaches, Catholics claim they are Catholics. Lapsed Catholic is, in this view, simply another way of being Catholic. Some say that such people are nominal Catholics, but that isn't quite right. "Nominal" has to do with names, as in "denominational," and Catholics do not think of the Church as a denomination. The Jewish comic Lenny Bruce once observed, "The Catholic Church is the church we mean when we say 'church.'" Certainly it is the church that Catholics mean when they say "church." Catholic is a communal and sacramental given, not a choice. In sociological jargon, it is an ascribed and not an elected identity. You cannot get away from it; at least not easily, and maybe not at all.

Of course, I am speaking mainly about those who are called "cradle Catholics." Converts are a different matter. Those who later in life are received into full communion with the Catholic Church often bridle at being called converts. When I was a Lutheran, evangelical Protestant friends would ask me when I was converted or born again; I answered that although I didn't personally remember it, I knew the exact time and place: when I was two weeks old at the baptismal font of St. John's Lutheran Church in Pembroke, Ontario. (More precisely, I'm told that I was baptized by my pastor father in the kitchen of the parsonage because my siblings had chicken pox and we were quarantined.) Better-informed Catholics well know that conversion is a life-long process of living out the grace received in baptism, yet the distinction between "converts" and "cradle Catholics" is deeply entrenched. Father (later Cardinal) Avery Dulles was one of my sponsors when I was received into full communion by the then archbishop of New York, John O'Connor. Dulles had been a nominal Presbyterian when, as a young man, he had been received some forty years earlier. "Get used to it," he told me, "no matter how long you live, to Catholics you will always be a convert priest." Not that I'm complaining, mind you.

A couple of years ago, Cardinal Dulles published a fine little introduction to Catholicism, *The New World of Faith*. A friend who is a cradle Catholic tells me he was not much taken with the book, and didn't quite know why. Then it struck him that Dulles, as an adult convert, treats Catholicism as a discovery; but for my friend the Church is the inherited and taken-for-granted reality. The Church is not the journey ahead but the place from which one begins. Moreover, Dulles writes about Catholicism as a "magnificent artifact" to be cherished and defended, whereas for my friend being Catholic is mainly a matter of, as he puts it, "negotiating an accommodation with the larger culture."

For Dulles, by way of contrast, that "larger culture" is the inherited and taken-for-granted reality; Catholicism is the new and challenging thing. The pastor of a neighboring parish tells me that he would not want a priest on his staff who does not read the *New York Times* every day. He said nothing about whether the priest should pray his office, the Liturgy of Hours, every day, or be familiar with the encyclicals and other teaching initiatives of the popes. Clearly, the pastor is in the mode of negotiating with the larger culture. It is not simply that one comment: The pattern of his conversation and life reflects a goal of rising above The Catholic Thing. The Catholic Thing is the problematic past, not the challenging future.

The dynamics involved are not necessarily peculiar to Catholicism. An agnostic friend who taught at an Ivy League university for years underwent a born-again experience under Baptist auspices. For his sabbatical year, he decided to accept an invitation to teach at an evangelical college. He discovered, he tells me, that the most self-consciously sophisticated of his evangelical colleagues were the most boringly parochial. They were touchingly eager to convince him and others that they were in conversation with what my friend viewed, and knew all too well, as the stiflingly parochial and achingly correct discourse of the Ivy League. They displayed, he said, a practiced aloofness, bordering on disdain, for the Baptist faith and life that was, for my friend, the bracing alternative to "the larger culture." One person's stifling ghetto is another's bracing alternative.

So it is with cradle Catholics, including many priests and academics, born into the all-embracing world of Catholicism. They know the inside stories, the flaws and foibles and legendary figures of the Church, and they can regale one another with the rich lore of miscreance and scandal. Catholicism is one big extended family with colorful ethnic subdivisions. Catholics of a certain age—those who can speak from personal experience about "the pre-Vatican II Church"—have tales beyond numbering of real or imagined instances of oppression, hypocrisy, pious pettiness, and intolerable constraints. Not surprisingly, in the company of such cradle Catholics, it is a mark of sophistication to have transcended "the Catholic ghetto." Dissent from official teachings—typically from teachings that do not sit well with the surrounding culture, and most typically from teachings touching on sexuality—is taken to be a mark of having grown up. The disposition is this: "Yes, I am a Catholic but I think for myself." The somewhat implausible assumption is that what one thinks up by oneself is more interesting than what the Church teaches.

It is true that, as the sixteenth-century St. Ignatius of Loyola put it, we should think with the Church *(sentire cum ecclesia)*. It is also true that thinking with the Church begins with thinking. Faithful assent is not a matter of standing to attention, clicking one's heels, and saluting at the appearance of every document from Rome. Rather, it is a matter of thinking for myself so that I can think with the Church, the prior assumption being that the Church possesses a teaching charism and authority that warrants my assent. I think for myself not to come up with my own teaching but to make the Church's teaching my own. That is not always easy to do. People say they have difficulty with one teaching or another. That is not necessarily a problem. The problem arises when we assume that the problem is with the teaching and not with ourselves. The great nineteenth-century theologian Cardinal John Henry Newman said, "Ten thousand difficulties do not add up to a doubt." We will have reason to come back to that wisdom later on.

There are no doubt unthinking Catholics. Asked what they believe, they say they believe what the Church believes, whatever that may be. But the authentic Catholic spirit is well expressed by the fifth-century St. Augustine: "No one believes anything unless one first thought it believable. Everything that is believed is believed after being preceded by thought. Not everyone who thinks believes, since many think in order not to believe; but everyone who believes thinks, thinks in believing and believes in thinking."

Those who think it is no big thing to dissent from or disagree with the Church's teaching often betray a touching, yet perverse, confidence in the Church that might be described as ecclesiastical fundamentalism. In this view, the fundamental realities that constitute the Church are so taken for granted that it is simply inconceivable that dissent or taking liberties at the edges could do any real damage. People who really do love the Church and think of it as their mother can be like adolescents trying to break loose from parental tutelage: There is a felt need to distance oneself from her confining embrace. They certainly mean her no real harm and, were she mortally threatened, they would come to her defense. But in the process of growing up and thinking for themselves, they may tell themselves and others that dear old mother has become a little dotty and is altogether too demanding. My friend who did not like the book by Cardinal Dulles would seem to be of this kind. He is put off by Dulles's discovery of Catholicism as a "magnificent artifact." For him, Catholicism is more in the nature of a family heirloom, a constellation of inherited beliefs and practices to be treated respectfully in the process of outgrowing it. It is hardly the exclusive gift of converts, but it may be easier for converts to share Cardinal Dulles's discovery of Catholicism as "the new world of faith."

We speak of people "converting to Catholicism," which is understandable enough. More accurately, one "enters into full communion" with the Church. To say that one enters into "full" communion implies that one is already in some kind of communion with the Church that is less than full. And that is exactly what the Catholic Church teaches. *Lumen Gentium* means "light to the nations," and that is the title of the important document of the Second Vatican Council on how the Catholic Church understands herself. The Council's document on Christian unity, *Unitatis Redintegratio*, says that all Christians who are baptized and believe in Jesus Christ as their Lord and Savior are "in a certain but imperfect communion" with the Catholic Church.

In this view, entering into full communion is a matter of bringing the imperfect to perfection. Other Christians may bridle at this. They don't think they are Catholics, and they don't take kindly to the Catholic Church's assumption that they really are Catholics, although imperfectly so. It is hard for Catholics to explain this teaching without giving offense. In our culture, it is polite to say that all religions are more or less equal. What matters is that your religion "works for you." Then the Catholic Church comes along and violates the protocols of polite society with this talk about perfect and imperfect, less full and more full, and even, if you would believe it, true and false. Just who does the Catholic Church think she is anyway?

Well, that *is* the question. She (note the feminine, for the Bible calls the Church "the bride of Christ" and brides are feminine) thinks she is the Church of Jesus Christ most fully and rightly ordered through time. That is, admittedly, a heavy-duty claim. Needless to say, not everybody accepts that claim. Not by a long shot. There are more than 2 billion Christians in the world, and over 1 billion of them Roman Catholic. That would seem to suggest that close to a billion Christians in the world do not accept the aforementioned claim. The Catholic Church is keenly aware of the awkwardness and potential offensiveness of maintaining the claim, but it really can't be helped. To use another image that occurs again and again in the New Testament, the Church is the body of Christ. There is only one Christ and therefore there can be only one body of Christ. There are many churches, but finally there is only one (upper case) Church. These teachings fall into the field of theology called ecclesiology, meaning what the Church believes about the Church, which is to say what she believes about herself.

As with every teaching of the Church, we haven't reached to the heart of the matter until we get to Christ. Put differently, ecclesiology and every other department of Catholic theology is finally christology, which means it has to do with what the Church believes about Christ. Bear with me here, for we are on the edge of deep waters. All Christians, if they really are Christians, have a relationship with Jesus Christ. If one is related to Christ, and if Christ is the head of the body, then one is in some very important sense related to the body of Christ, the Church. That is what is meant by certain but imperfect communion with the Church. In other words, Christ and the Church are coterminous. The Catholic Church readily recognizes, indeed celebrates, all the saving and sanctifying graces of God outside the Catholic Church. Many Christians who are not in full communion with the Church are more faithful and more holy than many who are in full communion. That is an undeniable fact of life, and a fact of life that has important theological implications.

The Catholic Church understands herself to be the gravitational center of the Christian movement through time. That may sound like unseemly boasting, but it is necessary to say it if, in fact, there is only one Christ and therefore only one Church. And so *Lumen Gentium* asserts that all the Christian grace to be found outside the formal boundaries of the Catholic Church gravitates toward unity with the Catholic Church. In John 17, Jesus prays for his disciples that "they may be one." He is praying that they may be *visibly* one, "so that the world may believe that you have sent me." The point is not to argue that all Christians should become Catholic. The point is to explain, all too briefly, how the Catholic Church thinks about these matters, and to explore some of the interesting questions raised by that way of thinking. If one believes that Christ intended a continuing community of disciples, and any fair-minded reading of the New Testament leaves no doubt that he did, it seems highly improbable that he did not have in mind a form that community should take. The gospel of Jesus Christ was not just a message dropped into the maelstrom of history, anyone and everyone being free to interpret the message and organize religious associations composed of those who agree with their interpretation.

The four gospel accounts are filled with instructions by Jesus about what the disciples are to do, and about what kind of community they are to be, after he has ascended to the Father. He chose apostles and, among the apostles, he chose Peter to be the center of unity. In the gospel accounts, Peter is always listed first. In the cupola above the altar of St. Peter's Basilica in Rome, written in Latin in letters six feet high, are the words of Jesus to Peter in Luke 22: "And you, when you are converted, strengthen your brethren." This is Peter's ministry of unity. Theologians of all Christian communities can agree that Jesus established what is called the "Petrine Ministry." Almost all Christians say in the Nicene Creed, "I believe in one, holy, catholic, and apostolic Church." But, of course, not all Christians agree on what is meant, either in theory or in practice, by an apostolic community united around Peter. Long before there was a book called the New Testament for Christians to disagree about, the early Church decided that the mark of continuity in Christian teaching and life is "apostolicity." The Church is identified by doctrine called apostolic, and also by persons who are apostles. In Ephesians 2, St. Paul writes about the Church as the fulfillment of the elect people of Israel: "So then you are no longer strangers and sojourners, but you are fellow citizens with the saints and members of the household of God, built upon the foundation of the apostles and prophets, Christ Jesus himself being the cornerstone."

What we today recognize as the Catholic Church obviously did not appear overnight. It is a long and complicated story, filled with heroic fidelity as well as villainy and intrigue, that brought the band of disciples who, in Jerusalem, first received the Holy Spirit on the day called Pentecost to today's Church of papal Rome with its thousands of bishops, hundreds of thousands of priests and religious ("religious" are nuns, monks, friars, and others vowed to the "consecrated life"), and more than a billion adherents around the world. But Catholics understand that it is the continuing story of "the household of God, built upon the foundation of the apostles and prophets, Christ Jesus himself being the cornerstone." By the end of the first century, the original apostles appointed by Jesus were dead or dying, and the Christian community understood that their authority now passed to their successors and to the local churches they had established. One cannot draw a neat and uncontested historical line between the apostolic "primacy" of St. Peter and the primacy of the current pope in Rome. But there is a clear line of apostolic authority. Clearer, at the very least, than any other line that can be drawn.

In the early centuries, there were tumultuous conflicts over heresies and countermovements. These conflicts were only gradually and with great difficulty resolved by bishops, who are the successors to the apostles, meeting in councils. There were numerous questions to be settled: Which writings that claimed to be apostolic were authentic and should be included in the collection (called the "canon") that we now recognize as the New Testament? That question was still being debated in the third century and beyond. Was Jesus true God and true man, the Second Person of the Holy Trinity and coequal with the Father and the Holy Spirit? Or was he only a God-like man, or maybe God in the disguise of humanity? The questions could hardly have been more fundamental, and they went to the heart of what Christians were to believe about God, human history, and the hope of salvation.

On the really big questions, such as the trinitarian nature of God and the deity of Christ, most Christians agree on what is called the Great Tradition, sometimes described as the consensus of the early Church. That is, most Christians accept as authoritative the first seven ecumenical or general councils, named after the cities in which the bishops met. (Nicea I in the year 325; Constantinople I, 381; Ephesus, 431; Chalcedon, 451; Constantinople II, 553; Constantinople III, 680 to 681; and Nicea II, 787.) After the division between East and West, meaning between Constantinople and Rome, toward the end of the first millennium, the Catholic Church in the West recognized fourteen more councils, all the way through the Second Vatican

Council, held from 1962 to 1965. Over time, appeal was increasingly made to the authority of the pope to convene councils and settle disputes. As successor to Peter as the bishop of Rome, he exercised the Petrine Ministry. ("Pope," by the way, simply means *papa*. That is why he is addressed as "Holy Father." He is the earthly head of the Catholic family.)[4]

How does one locate in time and place the Catholic Church? Answer: The Catholic Church is all the people who are in communion with a bishop who is in communion with the bishop of Rome. As we have seen, many Christians live outside the formal boundaries of the Catholic Church. Most particularly, the Catholic Church recognizes the Christians of the East, commonly called Orthodox, as possessing all the marks of apostolicity, with the exception of not being in full communion with the Petrine Ministry. This, then, is what the Catholic Church means when she claims to be the Church of Jesus Christ most fully and rightly ordered through time. *Lumen Gentium*, the document of Vatican Council II mentioned earlier, says that the Church of Jesus Christ "subsists" in the Catholic Church. That is different from saying that the Catholic Church simply *is*—exclusively and without remainder—the Church of Jesus Christ. The bishops in council were quite deliberate in making the distinction between "subsists" and "is."[5] So the argument with respect to becoming Catholic goes like this: If Christ intended a definite "form" for his Church, and if one wants to be obedient to Christ's intention, then one should belong to the form of his Church that most fully embodies that intention.

Lumen Gentium, for all its ecumenical sensitivity, puts the matter straightforwardly: "Whosoever, therefore, knowing that the Catholic Church was made necessary by God through Jesus

Christ, would refuse to enter her or remain in her could not be saved." Thus do apparently arcane theological and historical considerations of ecclesiology arrive at a conclusion of utmost personal urgency. Going back to the church fathers of the early centuries and continuing today, the Church teaches that "outside the Church there is no salvation" *(extra ecclesiam nulla salus)*. The Catholic *Catechism* immediately adds, "This affirmation is not aimed at those who, through no fault of their own, do not know Christ and his Church." It is not said today in polite company, but Catholics used to excuse good Christians who did not become Catholic by saying that they suffered from "invincible ignorance." It is not mere politeness, however, that keeps us from saying that all who disagree with us on this great question are invincibly ignorant. Christians who are not Catholics are not *extra ecclesiam;* they are in a "certain but imperfect communion with the Church." Their entering into full communion depends upon their "knowing" that the Catholic Church is what she claims to be.

A non-Catholic Christian may say, "I do not know that. I am not persuaded that it is true." Maybe it is his fault that he does not know. Maybe he has not given it sufficient thought or is guilty of resisting the evidence. On the other hand, perhaps the evidence and argument have not been presented persuasively. But the teaching of the Church is unambiguous: If one knows the truth, if one is persuaded of the truth and yet freely and knowingly refuses to act on the truth, then one is culpable, and the stakes could not be higher. Finally, the decision of whether or not to become Catholic is a matter of conscience—meaning a conscience informed by a conscientious search for the truth. Need I add that some of the finest Christians I know are not

Catholics? That in no way diminishes the urgency of being in full communion with the Church of Jesus Christ most fully and rightly ordered through time.

A great untold story is the number of adults, in America and the world, who are becoming Catholic. Catholics used to relish "conversion stories" and, truth to tell, most of them still do, but in these "ecumenical" times they feel a little guilty about it. Of course there are also many who are, to all practical purposes, leaving the Church. Are there as many or more going out the back door as are entering at the front door? We do not know, in part because there is no formal rite for leaving as there is for entering. All the evidence suggests that the overwhelming majority of "lapsed" Catholics still think they are Catholics. As it is said, "Once a Catholic, always a Catholic." And the Church agrees. Unless they have formally renounced the faith and committed apostasy, they are still Catholics. Very bad Catholics perhaps, but Catholics nonetheless. They are indelibly marked by baptism; the sign of the cross traced on their heads and their hearts cannot be erased. The life of a lapsed Catholic is frequently characterized by the time lapsed before he returns to the mother he neglected but never forgot.

Returning to the question of conversions, in recent years in the United States alone about 200,000 adults each year enter into full communion with the Catholic Church. That is in addition to the more than one million infant baptisms each year, and the arrival of millions of Hispanic, mainly Mexican, immigrants, legal and otherwise. The official count of Catholics in America is somewhat over 65 million. Our interest at the moment, however, is in the adult converts. The 200,000 are more or less evenly divided between those who are received by baptism and those who were baptized in other Christian communities. The former are called "catechumens," the latter "candidates." The former are becoming Christians and the latter are becoming more fully the Christians they were. The number of adult converts has been growing, no doubt in part because of the success of the Rite of Christian Initiation of Adults (RCIA), a program of evangelization and instruction begun after the Second Vatican Council.

If one asks why the untold story of adult converts remains untold, I expect one important reason is that it does not fit the usual ways of describing the Catholic circumstance in America. As with any family, Catholics are beset by family quarrels. There are "liberals" and "conservatives," "progressives" and "traditionalists," to mention but the most common of partisan labels. All of them, for their reasons and to their own ends, tend to depict a Church that is embattled, besieged, and struggling to survive. Here is Peter Steinfels of the *New York Times* in his recent book on Catholicism, *A People Adrift*: "Today the Roman Catholic Church in the United States is on the verge of either an irreversible decline or a thoroughgoing transformation." That's the opening line on which the next four hundred pages are a dispirited riff. The same theme is promulgated by authors on the conservative side of the aisle. Whether from the left or from the right, all have proposals for change that will, or so it is said, revitalize a Church in unprecedented crisis. The crisis, in the usual telling of the story, is perpetually unprecedented. It does not fit the purposes of such authors to pay much attention to the 200,000 adults per year who are becoming Catholics. That is at least one reason the story remains untold.

It is not that most Catholics are not "convert-minded." They are. In my experience, devout Catholics typically have a little list of people for whom they are praying that they will "come into the Church." There is a public reticence about this, however. Evangelical Protestants come right out and ask, "Are you saved?" It takes a very special circumstance for a Catholic to ask someone, "Why aren't you a Catholic?" There are several reasons for Catholic reticence. First, Catholics do not believe that everyone who is not a Catholic or, for that matter, not a Christian, is missing out on eternal salvation. One reason they don't believe that is because the Church does not teach that. *Lumen Gentium* again: "Those who, through no fault of their own, do not know the Gospel of Christ or his Church, but who nevertheless seek God with a sincere heart, and, moved by grace, try in their actions to do his will as they know it through the dictates of their conscience—those, too, may achieve eternal salvation." The rule is that God denies nobody, absolutely nobody, the grace necessary for salvation. What they do with that grace is another matter.

Then there is the question of conscience. Catholics are insistent on the importance of acting according to conscience. Conscience must not be pressured or bullied. Many people, and no doubt many Catholics as well, mistakenly think that acting according to conscience means doing what you want, what you feel like doing. With respect to a proposed course of action, the question is asked, "Are you comfortable with that?" But acting in conscience is not a matter of what we feel like doing or what makes us comfortable. Conscience is the God-given capacity to discern the truth and act upon it, which is sometimes exceedingly uncomfortable. Developing what St. Paul says in the second chapter of Romans about the law written on our hearts, the Second Vatican Council puts it this way: "Deep within his conscience man discovers a law which he has not laid upon himself but which he must obey. Its voice, ever calling him to love and to do what is good and to avoid evil, sounds in his heart at the right moment . . . For man has in his heart a law inscribed by God. His conscience is man's most secret core and his sanctuary. There he is alone with God whose voice echoes in his depth."

In his *Letter to the Duke of Norfolk,* John Henry Newman defended Catholics against the charge that they surrender their conscience to the authority of the Church. "Conscience is a messenger of Him who, both in nature and in grace, speaks to us behind a veil, and teaches and rules us by his representatives. Conscience is the aboriginal Vicar of Christ." The title "Vicar of Christ" is, of course, one of the many titles given the pope. Newman's point is that the original Vicar of Christ, prior in time and authority, is conscience. This, too, is part of what is meant when we say that "thinking with the Church" *(sentire cum ecclesia)* begins with thinking. Conscience is a truth-seeking capacity. It is our duty not only to have a conscience formed and informed by the truth but also to act always according to conscience. Among the reasons for the reticence of Catholics in working to convert others is respect for the "most secret core and sanctuary" of the other, which is conscience. Thus the work of conversion is in largest part the hard work of prayer for others, along with the delicate dropping of clues to the truth that the well-ordered conscience is seeking.

There are other reasons for reticence, some of them less elevating. As noted before, Catholics, too, are infected by the religious relativism of the surrounding culture in which it is assumed that religion is not a matter of what is true or false but of what works for you. Also, unlike many Protestant churches, and especially unlike evangelical churches, Catholic clergy and parishes seldom conduct aggressive programs of evangelizations aimed at gaining new members. One decidedly nontheological reason for this is that most priests think they already have more people than they are able to serve. Evangelical "megachurches" are defined as those with two thousand or more members. The *average* Catholic parish in the United States has two thousand members, many of them in large urban areas have 15,000 or more, and only two or three priests on staff. Suggest to the pastor of such a parish that he should embark upon a program to gain new members and he may well think that is the last thing he needs.

Reticence and hesitancy about conversion is also the product of long memories about Catholicism's uncertain place in an overwhelmingly Protestant country. Anti-Catholicism has a long and vicious history in America, and is today by no means a thing of the past. Enemies of the Church—and "enemies" is definitely the right word—accused Catholics of planning a "takeover" of Protestant America. In response, many Catholics maintained a low public profile, and still today are not disposed to trumpet the rapid growth of the Church. Moreover, and this is somewhat more complicated, there is the matter of ecumenism. Vatican II irrevocably committed the Catholic Church to the quest for Christian unity, and many Catholics sense a tension, even a contradiction, between ecumenism and conversions. I regularly hear complaints from people who made inquiries about becoming Catholic only to be discouraged or turned away by priests who told them that conversion is passé "in this ecumenical age." As we have seen, that is definitely not the teaching of the Church, but many Catholics have in a few decades gone from believing that non-Catholics are headed for Hell to wondering why anybody should want to become a Catholic. It is said that a certain distortion of ecumenism has produced the ecumaniac. An ecumaniac is defined as someone who loves every church but his own.

These, then, are some of the factors contributing to a wide-spread Catholic ambivalence about converts and conversion. Truth to tell, however, my experience suggests that most Catholics are less ambivalent than they seem. They have that little list of people who, they pray, will enter the Church; and when someone does, there is rejoicing over the lost sheep that has been found. There is no doubt a tribal element in seeing someone "come over to our side," especially if that someone is a person of some prominence. As a New York friend remarked of a noted Protestant pastor coming into the Church, "It's like the Yankees stealing a star pitcher from the Red Sox." Relatively few of the 200,000 who enter each year are people of public prominence, of course, and those who had not been baptized were not on the other side (meaning the Protestant side) to begin with. Nor is it true that all these people became Catholic as the result of careful theological deliberation about the Church most fully and rightly ordered through time. Far from it. Although we lack scientific studies of the phenomenon, the evidence suggests that many thousands enter into full communion with the Church because they want to be in full communion with husbands or wives or children who are in full communion with the Church. Some may say that is a "nontheological" reason for becoming Catholic. But those who say that, I believe, have a deficient theology of the myriad and mysterious ways in which God's grace works in human lives.

Becoming a Catholic is not always easy. Anecdotal evidence, supported by formal studies, indicates that many catechumens and candidates are put off by their experiences with RCIA. A recent study by the bishops conference, "Journey to the Fullness of Life," suggests that RCIA, too often dumbed down, pays minimal attention to doctrine, which is, after all, what the Church actually teaches about faith and life. RCIA sessions usually begin in the early fall; the climax in baptism or reception comes at the Great Vigil of Easter. A medical doctor and former Methodist who signed up with RCIA tells me this of his experience: "The sister leading the sessions is so excruciatingly ecumenical that we spend more time on other religions and Christian denominations than on Catholic teaching. Finally several of us had to tell her that we were there to become Catholics. As wonderful as those other religious communities may be, we had been there and done that." Another candidate laments that her RCIA experience was more about "telling our stories" and the marvels of "communal bonding" than about Catholic faith. When she raised questions prompted by her reading of the *Catechism of the Catholic Church*, she was politely informed that the *Catechism* is "awfully propositional" and "we are beyond that here."

More poignant is the story of a nominally Episcopalian business executive who for more than twenty years had fervently longed to be united with her Catholic husband in receiving Holy Communion. Finally, a friend helped her overcome some major objections she had long held against Catholicism and she joined an RCIA class. So eagerly, so yearningly, was she looking forward to the time when she and her husband would be one in the Eucharist, which the Church teaches is the "source and summit" of the Christian life.

Then, halfway through the RCIA course, she attended a wedding in a Catholic parish. The very congenial priest invited everyone present, including Protestants and probably people who had not been baptized, to come forward and receive Holy Communion. "There I was," she says, "preparing to enter the Catholic Church, the most momentous decision of my life, and there was this priest happily handing out the body of Christ to anyone and everyone as though he was distributing Oreo cookies." It is not always easy. Flannery O'Connor, that great Catholic novelist, said that we often have to suffer more from the Church than for the Church. And yet, despite all, hundreds of thousands continue to be drawn to the gravitational center of the Christian reality, the Church of Jesus Christ most fully and rightly ordered through time.

2 | Becoming the Catholic I Was

My own story of becoming Catholic is probably not representative. But then, whose is? For thirty years I had been a Lutheran pastor, theologian, and writer. Thirty years is a long time. I did not act precipitously. I suppose that, were I to give a title to my story, it would be "Becoming the Catholic I Was." I was received on the feast of the Nativity of Mary—September 8, 1990—by Cardinal John O'Connor, then Archbishop of New York. The Cardinal and I had been friends for years, and we had worked together on various projects of mutual interest. He had frequently said on public occasions that he hoped I would never become a Catholic because the Church needed Protestant friends. But we both knew that he said that tongue in cheek, and he made no attempt to disguise his pleasure in receiving me into full communion. The Cardinal, may he rest in peace, had a greatly exaggerated view of the contribution I would bring to the Church. As for me, the gift was entirely one-sided, and I was the recipient.

It happened in the small chapel of the Cardinal's residence at 451 Madison Avenue, a chapel dedicated to St John the Evangelist. My sponsors were Father (later Cardinal) Avery Dulles and George Weigel, the Catholic writer and biographer of John Paul II, both dear friends of many years. After the rite of confirmation and reception, Cardinal O'Connor hosted a most convivial dinner, and a fine time was had by all. As I left the residence later that evening, I asked Dulles what he thought of the event. Remembering his reception into the Church decades earlier, he responded in his smilingly angular way, "You know what I missed? I missed the retractions, recantations, and anathemas against your former heresies." Needless to say, he had been received before Vatican II and the dawning of the ecumenical era.

Although I had told close friends about my decision to "swim the Tiber," many learned about it by way of an extended report in the *New York Times*. I issued a short statement explaining what I was doing and why. With Lutheran friends especially in mind, the statement concluded: "To those of you with whom I have traveled in the past, know that we travel together still. In the mystery of Christ and his Church, nothing that is good and true is lost, and the broken will be mended. If, as I am persuaded, my communion with Christ's Church is now the fuller, then it follows that my unity with all who are in Christ is now the stronger. We travel together still." When a year later, again on the Nativity of Mary, Cardinal O'Connor, assisted by a host of bishops, archbishops, and priests, ordained me a priest of the Catholic Church, he read that statement again. With a few notable exceptions, my friendships with Lutherans, as well as with other Protestants and Orthodox, have remained intact. Most said they understood why I did what I did; many were and are thinking hard about doing the same; and some have since entered into full communion.

When John Henry Newman was asked at a dinner party why he became a Catholic, he responded that it was not the kind of thing that could adequately be explained between the soup and fish courses. I do not presume to compare myself to the great Cardinal Newman. Yet anybody, or at least anybody in the English-speaking world, who sets out on this path cannot be unaware of Newman's companionship along the way. When asked the same question, and, of course, one is regularly asked, I usually refer to Newman's response. But then I add what I call the short answer, which is simply this: I became a Catholic in order to be more fully what I was and who I was as a Lutheran. I became a Catholic when I discovered that I could no longer persuasively explain to others or to myself why I was not a Catholic. The story that follows may shed some light on that too short response.

In the statement before my reception, I also said:

I cannot express adequately my gratitude for all the goodness I have known in the Lutheran communion. There I was baptized, there I learned my prayers, there I was introduced to Scripture and creed, there I was nurtured by Christ on Christ, there I came to know the utterly gratuitous love of God by which we live astonished. For my theological formation, for friendships beyond numbering, for great battles fought, for mutual consolation in defeat, for companionship in ministry— for all this I give thanks. . . . As for my thirty years as a Lutheran pastor, there is nothing in that ministry that I would repudiate, except sins and shortcomings. My becoming a priest in the Roman Catholic Church will be the completion and right ordering of what was begun all those years ago. Nothing that is good is rejected, all is fulfilled.

Begin with St. John's Lutheran Church in the Ottawa Valley of Ontario, Canada. We were eight children, six boys and two girls, and our father was the pastor of St. John's, which belonged to the Lutheran Church—Missouri Synod. The Missouri Synod was and is the more conservative Lutheran body, as distinct from the larger Evangelical Lutheran Church in America (ELCA). These two bodies, and a few smaller ones, account for about 8 million Lutherans in the United States. Polling data indicate that many more identify themselves as Lutheran but are not listed by the Lutheran denominations. Lutherans, who are overwhelmingly German and Scandinavian in background, tend to keep a low public profile. Garrison Keillor's depiction of the Lutherans of Lake Wobegon in his popular radio show "The Prairie Home Companion" exaggerates this tendency, but not by much. An essay in *First Things* by Matthew Rose, a young Lutheran theologian, describes the Lutheran sensibility with considerable insight and self-effacing humor:

"When given the option," Garrison Keillor tells us, "Lutherans will always downsize." So far as I can tell, personal "downsizing" is the only way to make sense of what historian Mark Noll fairly calls the "remarkably unremarkable" story of American Lutherans. Such a quip shouldn't be anywhere near surprising, let alone offensive, to

most of us Lutherans. In fact we probably take "remarkably unremarkable" to be an almost cheery assessment of our famously phlegmatic lives. Such modesty ranks right up there with our other virtues: constancy, candor, and an affinity for things commonplace and unaffected. Outré we are not.

A built-in aversion to popularity seems to be Lutherans' animating instinct. It's a soundly orthodox one too, most of us think. For all their irresistible silliness, the pious inhabitants of Keillor's Lake Wobegon certainly have one thing right—all things being equal, Lutherans prefer to be as unassuming as humanly possible. In the annals of American history, we've garnered precious little main text; we're the cultural equivalent of a buried footnote.

How Lutherans have managed to dodge the limelight of so many American historical moments is truly astounding. You might say that the tone was set as far back as 1565, when explorer Pedro Menendez razed a Huegenot settlement and hanged its misidentified inhabitants as "Lutherans." At times, we've had a membership larger than the Episcopalians, Presbyterians, Congregationalists, Disciples, and Quakers combined, yet our history has been less noticeable than the Unitarians'. (If orthodox Christian historians have judged Unitarians as unfortunately famous, we've been justly dubbed famously unfortunate.) Our newsworthy potential, it's been pithily said, has been "not very great." . . . We have very little to brag about as far as "movers and shakers" go, a category about which we are naturally suspicious. I'd like to say that Lutherans are busy instead with the silent labor of life, but that sounds too pretentious for Lutheran sensibilities.

That describes a great deal of the Lutheranism of my childhood. In addition, however, the Missouri Synod wing of Lutheranism was, and is, famously contentious. In the early 1970s, there was a nasty division in the synod over disputes that need not delay us here, and I spent my last Lutheran years as a pastor of the ELCA, the sector of Lutheranism that is moving with astonishing alacrity into the orbit of oldline liberal Protestantism.

But it all began with St. John's Lutheran Church in Pembroke, Ontario, Canada. There was another dimension to being Lutheran, at least as I experienced it. To be brought up in that religious world was to know oneself as an *ecclesial* Christian. Of course, I did not put it that way as a boy, nor was it put that way to me, but I would in retrospect see what had happened. By an ecclesial Christian I mean someone who understands with mind and heart, and even feels with his fingertips, that Christ and his Church, head and body, are inseparable. For the ecclesial Christian, the act of faith in Christ and the act of faith in the Church are not two acts of faith but one. In the words of the third-century St. Cyprian, the martyr bishop of Carthage, "He who would have God as his Father must have the Church as his mother." In an important sense, every Christian, even those of the most individualistic habits of mind, is an ecclesial Christian because no one knows the gospel except he learn it from the Church. *Extra ecclesia nulla salus*—no salvation outside the Church—applies to all. For some, that truth seems incidental; for the ecclesial Christian it is constitutive, the very core, of faith and life.

Much later, when I was at college and seminary, I would avidly, almost voraciously, read the writings of Dietrich Bonhoeffer. His *Cost of Discipleship* and *Life Together* are high on the list of books I continue to recommend to all who are serious about living Christianly. Few thinkers have so profoundly formed my admittedly inadequate understanding of what it means to be a Christian. Students of Bonhoeffer have found in his *Ethics* and writings on the Church suggestions that he was on his way to becoming a Catholic. Whether or not they are right, that was not to be. Bonhoeffer was a Lutheran pastor, born in 1906, who early on joined the Christian opposition to the Nazi regime in Germany. For his part in rescuing Jews and in the plot to assassinate Hitler, he was hanged on the direct orders of Hitler only a few days before the end of World War II, on April 9, 1945. He was thirty-nine years old.

Years earlier, on Sunday, July 29, 1928, the young Bonhoeffer preached on what St. Paul says about the body of Christ in I Corinthians 12. He began his sermon this way:

> *There is a word that, when a Catholic hears it, kindles all his feeling of love and bliss; that stirs the depths of his religious sensibility from dread and awe of the Last Judgment to the sweetness of God's presence; and that certainly awakens in him the feeling of home; the feeling that only a child has in relation to its mother, made up of gratitude, reverence, and devoted love; the feeling that overcomes one when, after a long absence, one returns to one's home, the home of one's childhood. And there is a word that to Protestants has the sound of something infinitely commonplace, more or less indifferent and superfluous, that does not make their heart beat faster; something with which a sense of boredom is so often associated, or which at any rate does not lend wings to our religious*

feelings—and yet our fate is sealed if we are unable again to attach a new, or perhaps a very old, meaning to that word. Woe to us if that word does not become important to us again and soon. The word to which I refer is "Church," the meaning of which we propose to look at today.[1]

Bonhoeffer was an ecclesial Christian. As a youngster, perhaps at age twelve or so, I read reflections by O. P. Kretzman, then president of Valparaiso University, a Lutheran school in Indiana. He wrote, as I now recall it, "In this would my life be fulfilled, if by it I had lighted one candle at the shrine of Holy Mother Church." A bit on the sentimental side, one might now think, but then my heart burned within me. This was the great thing, to be enlisted in a grand cause, and the Church was that grand cause.

For Lutherans in this country, but also in Germany and Scandinavia, there has long been a minority "high church" party. Those who identify with it call themselves "evangelical catholics" in a manner similar to the Anglo-Catholic movement that was launched by Newman and others in nineteenth-century Anglicanism. The seemingly endless quest is for a way of being catholic without being uppercase Catholic. For Lutherans, this means emphasizing the continuity rather than discontinuity between medieval Catholicism and the sixteenth-century Reformation led by Martin Luther. The insistence is that the Lutheran Reformation was originally a movement of gospel reform within the one Church; there was no intention of forming a separated Lutheran Church. The schism of the sixteenth century was, in the words of the historian Jaroslav Pelikan, a Lutheran who later became Orthodox, a "tragic necessity."[2] I was keenly aware of the tragedy but never convinced of the necessity. As a Lutheran and evangelical catholic, I wrote over the years that our goal must be "the healing of the breach of the sixteenth century between Rome and the Reformation." The seeds of this conviction were sown back there in St. John's Lutheran Church of Pembroke, Ontario.

In my childhood experience, seemingly little things made a big difference. They might be called "nontheological" factors, but they were freighted with theological significance. Across the street from the parsonage of St. John's was an evangelical Protestant church named Zion and associated with the Christian and Missionary Alliance. Also across the street, next door to Zion, lived my best friends, the Spooner brothers, who, with their devoutly Catholic family, attended St. Columkil's Cathedral. It was unarticulated, but I am sure it was self-evident to me by the time I was eight years old that St. John's and the Catholic cathedral had more in common with each other than either one had with Zion.

For one immeasurably momentous thing, our churches baptized babies, and they believed that baptism worked a great change—indeed a saving change—in those babies. For another thing, a friend who went to Zion talked a lot about being saved. The Spooner boys and I found that a little strange and off-putting. Our being saved was something that God did through His Church; it was a given, a gift. And if being saved tended toward being taken for granted, it also had nothing of the sweated anxiety that it had for Dougy, our evangelical friend. Of course, I had never heard the Latin phrase *ex opere operato*—loosely translated as "from the thing done"—but, when I came across it years later, I recognized it as what I had always believed. Grace is bestowed by things done, mainly by sacramental things done. There is an objectivity to the gift given. Salvation is not a matter of seeking certainty in sorting through one's feelings and spiritual experiences. Salvation is saying yes to the gift given.

Unlike my Catholic friends, I was in catechism class taught to speak of *sola gratia*—"grace alone," which is one of the defining themes of the Reformation tradition. My father taught the class, which was held in the church basement, on Saturday mornings. One began "Saturday school" at age ten; the classes led four years later to the rite of confirmation at age fourteen, at which point one was first admitted to Holy Communion. The text for Saturday school was Martin Luther's *Small Catechism*, which included extended explanations authorized by the Missouri Synod. (The catechism was similar in format, but, needless to say, not always in content, to the *Baltimore Catechism* familiar to Catholics of an older generation, although the *Small Catechism* contained much more doctrinal and biblical elaboration.) We went through the *Catechism* once in the first two years and then again in the second two years, by which time we were expected to have it memorized in preparation for the public examination in front of hundreds of members of the congregation. As for *sola gratia*, I think I was more impressed by the *gratia* than by the *sola*. After all, we were expected to do something, to say yes, and to live as though we meant it.

In catechism class I was taught that the crucial distinction between Catholics and us is that we try to be good in gratitude for being saved, while Catholics try to be good in order to be saved. They were guilty of "works righteousness"—trying to please God by their good deeds—while we believed in *sola gratia*. As best I recall, I thought the supposedly crucial distinction was pretty much a distinction without a difference. It seemed obvious that my Catholic friends and I believed that we were baptized children of God for whom Christ died, and that it was very ungrateful and very dangerous to get on God's wrong side. I was taught that Catholics were more afraid that God would punish them for their sins; but we, being sure of forgiveness, were certain of our salvation. I was also taught, somewhat contradictorily, that Catholics sinned more casually because they could so easily go to confession and have their sins automatically forgiven by the priest.

I more or less dutifully learned these lessons but, between my Catholic friends and us, I did not notice much difference in the ways we feared punishment, casually sinned, and were sure of God's love. I do not wish to make light of the important questions entailed in formulas such as *sola gratia* and *sola fides* (faith alone); they are questions that have engaged serious theologians for centuries. In later chapters, we will see that these questions have an important place in today's quest for Christian unity. Here, however, I am reflecting on a Lutheran childhood and how I became the Catholic I was.

I do not wish to give the impression that I was theologically precocious as a little boy. I was not even especially devout. I really did not like having to go to church. During Dad's very long sermons, sometimes carefully crafted but delivered in a dispassionate monotone, I counted the number of bald heads in the congregation, or the squares on the ceiling high above, until I dozed off. But I am looking back now, trying to understand the formation of an ecclesial Christian—a Christian of lowercase catholic sensibilities on his way, step by step, to uppercase Catholic allegiance. There were other seemingly little things.

St. John's had a high altar, as did the other Lutheran churches I knew. As did the Catholic cathedral. On the few occasions I ventured to peek into the cathedral, however, I saw there were also statues of saints, and flickering votive lights, and, most impressively, the Real Presence of Jesus in the tabernacle above the high altar. When the people were not present for Sunday morning service, St. John's was behind its locked doors an empty auditorium awaiting its next use. But the cathedral was sacred space. Its doors were always open and, scattered about in what seemed to me the vast and darkened space, there were a few people praying and saying the rosary. They and what they were doing did not make the space sacred. They were drawn to a space made sacred by an other, by Another. There one was encountered by a Presence not of our pious creation. It was objective, it was given, it was real. It did not need or require anybody's agreement in order to be. *Ex opere operato.*

Catholicism, I early intuited, was *more.* There were other ways in which our church and their church were alike and yet different. From this distance in time, I risk exaggerating what I discerned then, but of this I am sure: What we believed and did was somehow dependent upon and drawn from what they believed and did. Catholicism was the source, and Catholicism was more. We both had communion rails at the altar, and at St. John's we knelt and received what we were taught was really and truly and without equivocation the Body and Blood of Christ. But we had "Communion service" only on one Sunday a month, recently increased from four times a year. They had Mass every week and even, I was told, every day. I was taught that receiving Communion too often would make it mean less, but it seemed to mean more to them.

We had the same little wafer-like hosts of bread and we used real wine. But after the Communion service, Dad put the left-over hosts and wine that had been consecrated on the altar back into the box and back into the bottle with the hosts and wine that had not been consecrated. They were no longer the Body and Blood of Christ. They were once again ordinary bread and ordinary wine. Had they, then, ever really changed? *Really?* Or had they changed only for a brief time by our believing that they had changed? Did it all come back to us, to me, what I believed, what I felt? At the cathedral, the priest consumed the last of the wine; the consecrated hosts he put in the tabernacle. Where is Jesus? He is *there.* In the tabernacle. Really. That putting of the leftover elements back into the box and the bottle. Such a little thing. Such a big thing.

A young American poet, Patrick Miller, catches the matter nicely:

The Real Presence

Present me with something real,
and nothing short of breath,
that inspiration may succeed,
and spirit conquer death:
something I might split in two
while always keeping one,
lying not beyond my touch,
nor doing would be done.

There were other big/little and little/big things. Other Protestant churches displayed a plain cross. We, like the Catholics, had a crucifix on the altar. On the cross, Christ was stretched in his suffering. Many years later, I was on a program with a famous evangelist from California who had built a huge "Crystal Cathedral" designed by a famous architect. He said there had been a debate about whether the cathedral should have a cross. Some people thought the cross an excessively gloomy symbol. "I said that of course there will be a cross," declared the famous evangelist. "The cross is the sign of Christianity and we're a Christian church." Then he paused and announced with a triumphant smile, "But I can tell you that there's nothing downbeat about the cross at Crystal Cathedral." An upbeat cross? Back in Pembroke, a Wesleyan church visited by our elementary school class had in large letters above the communion table, "He is not here. He is risen." Yes, I thought, he was not there.

In addition to the crucifix on the altar, Lutheran churches, like Catholic churches, had a cross on the top of their steeples. Protestant churches had a weather vane or nothing at all. In catechism class it was explained that the weather vane indicated that they were, in St. Paul's words to the Ephesians, "carried about by every wind of doctrine." We, on the other hand, were grounded in a strong doctrinal tradition. I was told, of course, that we believed in the Reformation's rule of *sola scriptura* (Scripture alone), but it was also evident that Scripture was never alone. Why else, just for starters, Luther's *Small Catechism*? The Spooner brothers and I both knew we had a Magisterium, an authoritative teaching office, although I'm sure I never heard the word as a boy. When it came to settling questions in dispute, they had the pope—and we had the faculty of Concordia Seminary in St. Louis, a school I would attend much later in life. Concordia was the Magisterium of Missouri

Synod Lutheranism. It seemed quite natural to inquire about "our position" on this or that. The "our" in the question self-evidently referred to the Missouri Synod, and the answer was regularly provided by a Concordia faculty member in the synod's official publication, *The Lutheran Witness*. The Missouri Synod had an answer to just about any question you could think to ask. And every answer was surrounded by a praetorian guard of biblical citations. So it was *sola scriptura* after all, as correctly interpreted by the Magisterium.

Why the Spooners went to one church and we to another seemed obvious enough: They were Catholics and we were Lutherans. They were taught that they belonged to the "one true Church." I was taught that I belonged to the Missouri Synod which, along with all who were in complete doctrinal agreement with the Missouri Synod, made up "the true visible Church on earth." Between their ecclesiological claims and ours, it was pretty much of a toss-up. They were taught that, despite my not belonging to the one true Church, I could still be saved by virtue of my "invincible ignorance." I was taught that people who did not belong to the true visible Church on earth, *even* Catholics, could be saved by virtue of—in the marvelous phrase of Francis Pieper, Missouri's preeminent theologian—a "felicitous inconsistency." These fine distinctions, too, I would learn later in life.

When we were boys about, say, twelve years old, I doubt whether the Spooners ever for a moment thought that maybe they should be Lutheran. I thought about what it would be like to be Catholic. I did not think about it very seriously, certainly not obsessively, but I thought about it. It seemed that, of all the good things we had, they had more. In addition, I knew where the good things we had came from. They came from the Church that had more. Martin Luther had been a Catholic. We were also taught, simultaneously and somewhat confusingly, both that he left and that he was excommunicated. The emphasis was on his leaving, however, his excommunication being depicted as little more than an after-the-fact gesture of papal pique. Much was made, however, of the difference between the Lutheran Reformation and the more radical Protestants whom the Lutherans called *Schwärmerei*, meaning religious zealots or enthusiasts. Religious enthusiasm, we were given to understand, was a bad thing. Witness those such as the Anabaptists, who had abandoned the baptism of babies, reduced the Lord's Supper to no more than a memorial meal, and condemned liturgy, stained-glass windows, and the historic calendar of the Church's year as remnants of "papism."

I do not recall anything in my boyhood that could aptly be described as anti-Catholicism. True, at Sunday dinners my father called the tail end of the chicken "the pope's nose," but it was said with a smile. Dad would go deer hunting with a local monsignor, and for the two of them deer hunting was pretty close to communion in sacred things *(communicatio in sacris)*. In the Missouri Synod of those days, praying with Catholics—or anyone else with whom we were not in "complete doctrinal agreement"—was condemned as "unionism." So perhaps Dad and the monsignor didn't pray up at the hunting camp. The rules didn't say anything about the deep communion of hunting together.

Of course, Catholics and Protestants attended different schools. The government of Ontario supported "separate" (meaning Catholic) schools and "public" (meaning Protestant) schools. Sometimes the Catholic kids would walk home from school on one side of the street shouting, "Catholic, Catholic ring the bell / Protestant, Protestant go to hell." To which we on the other side of the street reciprocated by reversing the jingle. It was all in good fun, much like a school cheer. I doubt whether even for a moment either of us thought it made serious reference to the other's eternal destiny. It was just the way things were.

There were other differences. For instance, my Catholic friends went to confession, and I was curious about that. "You mean you have to tell the priest *everything*?" I couldn't imagine confessing to my father, unless I got caught, as I frequently was. There was a pale ritual trace of confession at St. John's. The Lutheran doctrinal writings of the sixteenth century said that confession should be retained, maybe even as a sacrament. But four hundred years later, that had been reduced to people coming to the church on the Saturday before "communion Sunday" to "announce" their intention to receive the Lord's Supper. The idea was that the pastor would have an opportunity to counsel members who had spiritual problems. But, in practice, it was a simple matter of writing down their names in the "communion book," and, if Dad wasn't there to do it, my mother or one of my older siblings took over. "Taking announcements" was a regular family chore. I don't think I knew at the time that it was a vestige of what had once been the sacrament of penance, today called by Catholics the Sacrament of Reconciliation. (Actually, most Catholics still call it "going to confession.")

There was also the difference that the Cathedral of St. Columkil's had a bishop. He was put there, I was told, by the pope in Rome. St. John's had, well, my Dad. He got there, as he told the story, by a classmate who persuaded the congregation to call him as its pastor. By comparison with most Protestants, the Missouri Synod had a "high" view of the pastoral ministry. A pastor was not hired; he responded to a "divine call" from the congregation. Yet it is possible that I intuited early on that, between Bishop Smith and Dad, there was a qualitative difference of ecclesial dignity and authority. Not that I was at that early age inclined to doubt what Dad taught. After all, he had the Bible, Martin Luther, and the St. Louis faculty on his side. And he was indisputably authoritative, though not authoritarian, in manner. Not for nothing was he called "Pope Neuhaus" already during his seminary years. St. John's was one of the larger congregations in the Ontario District of the Missouri Synod, and Dad had a quasi-episcopal standing among the other Lutheran pastors. But he was not the Bishop of Pembroke, put there by the pope in faraway Rome.

I should add that this was not a matter of social status. The pecking order in Pembroke was unambiguously clear. The English and Scots, all solidly Protestant (mainly Anglican and Calvinist), owned and ran things. The German Lutherans were the solid working class. The Catholics were mainly French and, except for the Indians on the nearby reservation, were at the bottom of the social hierarchy. If thought that the Bishop Smith somehow outranked my Dad, it was in a different hierarchy, one that encompassed much more than Pembroke and questions of social status.

One summer, Bishop Smith was impolitic enough to criticize publicly the "godless" public schools. Dad was head of the public school board and sharply criticized the bishop in the *Pembroke Observer*. There followed various public exchanges, and the town was sharply divided along Catholic–Protestant lines. I had returned that summer from college in Texas to sell Fuller Brush products from door to door. I was known as one of "Pastor Neuhaus's boys," and wherever I went, I was met either with a warm welcome or with not-so-veiled hostility, depending on whether the house was Protestant or Catholic. I was proud of Dad's celebrity, but I secretly wondered about the soundness of his position. After all, at the dinner table I had heard Dad speak of the godless public schools. The Missouri Synod had, and still has, an extensive network of parochial schools, and it was Dad's great dream, never realized, to establish one at St. John's.

These were nontheological, even psychological, factors in the story of how I became the Catholic I was. That does not mean they were unimportant. I have long since given up all hope of definitive success in disentangling the factors that formed me from the intellectual and theological reasons I gave, and give, for the decisions I have made. Early on I came across and took to heart William Butler Yeats's caution against rummaging through the rag-and-bone shop of the human heart. Moreover, during my boyhood, the Protestant–Catholic difference was hardly experienced as a matter of life-or-death urgency. Except for occasional tribal disputes, live and let live was the order of the day. Where we differed, we were right and they were wrong, or at least it wasn't worth a fight. And, as I have said, our Lutheran differences with other Protestants on matters such as infant baptism and the Real Presence of Christ in Holy Communion were as sharp, if not sharper, than our differences with Catholics. Very early the seed was planted and grew into the firm intuition that we Lutherans were, come to the crunch, more on the Catholic side than the Protestant. Or at least we were supposed to be, and that made it problematic that we were, in fact, on the Protestant side. At seminary, I would read Peter Brunner, a notable Lutheran theologian in Germany. He said that one does not know what it means to be a Lutheran unless one asks every day why he is not a Catholic. That was an "Aha experience."

In any event, being brought up as a Missouri Lutheran—at least then and at least there—made me an ecclesial Christian. One might say a sacramental Christian or an incarnational Christian, but, whatever language is used, the deepest-down conviction, the most irrepressible sensibility, is that of the touchability, the visibility, the palpability, the communal instantiation of The Christian Thing. There is a marvelous phrase used by theologians in controversies over the nature of Christ's presence in the Eucharist: *Finitum capax infiniti*. It means "the finite is capable of the infinite." Put differently, there is no access to the infinite except through the finite. God's investment in the finite can be trusted infinitely.

Lutherans rejected the Catholic phrase *ex opere operato*. But surely, I thought, *ex opere operato* was in play when Martin Luther, in his ultimate defiance of Satan's every temptation, played his trump card: "I am baptized!" *Ex opere operato* is the sacramental enactment of *sola gratia*. It is relentlessly objective. By it, morbid introspection, the delusions of religious enthusiasm, and the deceptively clever postulations of the theological imagination are called to order by truth that is accountable to no higher truth. The One who is Truth speaks in the voice of the Church—"I baptize you"; "I forgive you your sins"; "This is my body."

It is true that in high school I had what evangelical Protestant friends would call a born-again experience. It was a church-related school in Seward, Nebraska, where I organized beer parties in the dormitory and led panty raids (an expression I haven't heard in decades) on the girls' dormitory. By comparison with the campus goings on of today, it all seemed quite innocent, but the school authorities took a dim view of the matter. I was given several weeks of "detention" in my room, which I could not leave except for classes and meals. One day, a young teacher came by to check on my spiritual well-being. I can recall the details with remarkable vividness as I write this so many years later. What he said was unremarkable. I had undoubtedly heard it thousands of times before. But now I heard it as if for the first time: "God is very disappointed with what you did, for He thinks so highly of you. But, because He loves you so much, He forgives you and will help you to be better."

How very conventional, one might well say. Pious banalities. Yet there and then I broke into tears of repentance and resolved that I would from that day on live to please the God who loved me so. I was fourteen years old then, and the resolution has been broken times beyond numbering. But for four or five days, maybe for a week after that encounter, I lived in an ecstatic state of the experienced immediacy of God's loving presence such as I have not known since. To this day, as I recall them, I draw on the experience of those days. To this day I am grateful for those days. In the years that followed I would, from time to time, try to re-create them, to experience again what I experienced then. It never worked. But I did later come across the words T. S. Eliot gives the martyred Thomas Becket in his *Murder in the Cathedral:* "I have had a tremor of bliss, a wink of heaven, a whisper, / And I would no longer be denied; all things / Proceed to a joyful consummation." Ah, yes, I thought, that is it. And I have thought so ever since.

The consequences of the experience also had a shadowed side. I, who had known ecstasy, was for a time contemptuous of the ritual and sacramental formalities of what I viewed as a spiritually comatose Lutheranism. For a time, I suppose, I might have been a good candidate for the Baptist ministry. I was becoming what in the Lutheran tradition is called a "pietist." Pietism, especially in the Missouri Synod, was viewed as a bad thing. It was depicted as a form of spiritual pathology that constructed one's relationship with God, even one's eternal salvation, on the foundation of spiritual experiences and living a holy life. Pietism was closely related to the errors of those whom Luther called the *Schwärmerei*, and similar to what Ronald Knox, in the Catholic tradition, would much later call "enthusiasm." After that encounter in Nebraska, and extending into my college years in Texas, I was, at least intermittently, a pietist. Missouri's animus toward pietism, I told myself and others, was an animus toward piety.

And it is true that during my childhood years the affective dimensions of Christian existence—the experienced reality of awe and wonder, of love and surrender—was suppressed, or at least never talked about. I cannot recall that anyone during those years ever discussed, or even mentioned, what is commonly referred to as a "religious experience." Religion was, above all, about subscribing to the right doctrines, then about going to church to hear the Word of God; in a third and subordinate place was morality, which meant at least staying out of trouble. Undue reference to the holiness of life smacked of "works righteousness." Works righteousness was the idea that one could get into the good graces of God by being a good person; it was the arch-heresy that negated the *sola gratia* and *sola fides*. Talking about personal religious experience, of an encounter with God, of love for Jesus—all that was frowned upon as self-dramatizing enthusiasm. Perhaps it is not surprising that, after having been to the mountaintop in the flatlands of Nebraska, I thought that Lutheranism was spiritually comotose.

During those college years, however, I was also embroiled in trying to sort out my subjective experience, my egotistic assertiveness, and my spiritual wishful thinking from the workings of grace. Maybe, I thought, the workings of grace were effected precisely through those dubious dynamics, or maybe I was just making up the Christian thing as I went along. It did not help when I stumbled across Kierkegaard's insistence that "purity of heart is to will one thing." To will one thing? Good luck with that. I fell back again and again on Luther's profound probings of the ambiguities of Christian existence. We are, he said, *simul iustus et peccator*—at the same time justified and sinful. The Christian life is the abandonment of the self, a ceasing to rummage through the rag-and-bone shop of the human heart, and a surrendering to a reckless reliance on the love of God in Christ mediated through "the means of grace"—Baptism, Word, and Lord's Supper. At times, and for long times, I really was a Lutheran. Not just denominationally.

Lutheran*ism* as a denomination, never mind as Church, was never very convincing. But Luther's radical construal of the gospel as unqualified grace—good works, feelings, and intellectual comprehension be damned—was, and still is for many, powerfully liberating. Those who have never been gripped by it cannot help but be scandalized by Luther's counsel, "Sin boldly." But for many it was, and is, the final, the unsurpassable, spiritual consolation. There was, however, the problem with Luther, as also with most forms of born-again Protestantism, that *sola gratia* always returns a person to, and too often never gets beyond, square one of the certainty of being saved. As a Lutheran theology professor of the time put it, "Growth in grace is a contradiction in terms." That, I thought, could not be right. If it were, there would be no saints. To which the Lutheran answer is that we are all saints. Well, yes; but if everybody is a saint, nobody is a saint. The fact of the Church's story, past and present, is that some do grow in grace, that they do move beyond square one, that they exemplify the possibilities of grace for which square one is the indispensable beginning—and the sure refuge in times of spiritual crisis.

I was vaguely searching for some way of holding together—for a synthesis, if you will—of gospel grace, of piety and devotion, of clear thinking, of moral progress, and, as I would slowly come to understand, ecclesial authority. At Concordia Theological Seminary in St. Louis, that way entered my life in the person of Professor Arthur Carl Piepkorn. Small of stature, Piepkorn combined a military bearing (he was a colonel in the army chaplain corps) with an impish manner. I was one of a small coterie of students who orbited about him, taking all his classes and meeting for weekly discussions at his home. We called him "the Pieps," although certainly not to his face, and American Lutherans who today describe themselves as "evangelical catholics"—perhaps as many as a fourth of the clergy—are known as Piepkornians. He was a man of intimidating erudition, deep piety, and disciplined prayer. He was something of a polymath, having earned doctorates in biblical archeology, medieval philosophy, and I don't know what else. He took unabashed delight in displaying his encyclopedic knowledge and provoking in others the joy of learning. In the 1930s, he was a leader in the Lutheran version of the liturgical renewal that was vibrantly contending for reform within Roman Catholicism, and he was among the pioneers of Lutheran–Roman Catholic theological dialogue following the Second Vatican Council. Moreover, he had a charming wife and three very attractive daughters, named Faith, Hope, and Charity. He was, all in all, a man in full.

Although he remained a Lutheran until his death, at age sixty-six, in 1973, Piepkorn gave me an understanding of Lutheranism that required my becoming Catholic. We are, he taught us, Christians first, catholic Christians second, Western catholic Christians third, and members of the Church of the Augsburg Confession fourth. That was, he said, the ordering of priorities in our ecclesial identity. To speak of "the Church of the Augsburg Confession"—referring to the 1530 Lutheran statement of faith at Augsburg, Germany—was to locate Lutheranism solidly within the history of the Church of the West. He insistently referred to the collection of sixteenth-century Lutheran doctrinal statements as "the symbolic books of the Church of the Augsburg Confession," thereby indicating that they were the "symbols" of a distinctive communion within the communion of the one, holy, catholic, and apostolic Church. Lutheranism was, in this view, a way of being catholic as the heirs of a Reformation tradition that was intended to be a movement of reform within and for the one Church of Christ. That intention tragically miscarried when Lutheranism became a separated ecclesial community. In more mischievous moods, Piepkorn suggested that it was Rome that separated itself from the authentic catholicity of the Church of the Augsburg Confession.

And so the theological stage was set for the prolonged drama of trying to be catholic without becoming uppercase Catholic. The invaluable contribution of Piepkorn was the understanding that Lutheranism is part of the tradition of the one Church. The accent was on continuity, not discontinuity. Unlike some other Protestants, the Lutheran Reformers had no delusions about being a new beginning by which the primitive and apostolic Church was reconstituted. Lutheranism was another chapter in the history of the one Church. The Church is not a theological school of thought or a society formed by adherence to theological formulas, not even formulas such as "justification by faith alone"; it is, rather, a historically identifiable apostolic community of discipleship through time, until the end of time. The fulfillment of the Reformation, therefore, is to bring its gifts into the mainstream of the continuing community from which it had been separated in the sixteenth century, mainly because of the obtuseness of Rome.

Some readers will no doubt recognize significant similarities with John Henry Newman and the "tractarian movement" of the nineteenth century. Newman and his colleagues attempted to reconstitute the Church of England as a middle way *(via media)* between liberal Protestantism and Roman Catholicism. In Anglicanism, the Thirty-Nine Articles as approved by Queen Elizabeth I in 1571 played a role similar to that of the sixteenth-century confessional writings in Lutheranism. The tractarians attempted to refashion Anglicanism in as catholic a manner as possible within the limits of the Thirty-Nine Articles. Until, in the famous Tract No. 90 of 1841, Newman turned things right side up—or, as his opponents insisted, upside down. Instead of their being the norm by which the whole of the catholic tradition is judged, said Newman, the Thirty-Nine Articles are to be judged by the whole of the tradition. Further, he argued that the Thirty-Nine Articles could be rightly interpreted as being compatible with the decrees of the sixteenth-century Council of Trent. Newman's position was roundly condemned by the Anglican establishment; two years later he would preach his celebrated sermon on "The Parting of Friends"; and on October 9, 1845, he was received into the Catholic Church.

In a very different time and circumstance, some of us who were evangelical catholics within Lutheranism would recognize the conclusion of the Augsburg Confession of 1530 as a kind of Tract No. 90. In that conclusion the signers at Augsburg declared:

> *Only those things have been recounted which it seemed necessary to say in order that it may be understood that nothing has been received among us, in doctrine or in ceremonies, that is contrary to Scripture or to the church catholic. For it is manifest that we have guarded diligently against the introduction into our churches of any new and ungodly doctrines.*

For us, that was understood to be a normative declaration; everything was to be held accountable to that claim. The question of what is normative for what, of which norm is trumps, has a long history of dispute. Between Scripture and tradition, many Protestants say Scripture is trumps; but they fail to take fully into account that the formula *sola scriptura*, and indeed Scripture itself, is part of the continuing tradition. Among liberal Protestants, many follow the twentieth-century theologian Paul Tillich in contending that "catholic substance" is to be held in tension with "Protestant principle." In this view, catholic substance is the received tradition and Protestant principle is the critique of that tradition. Protestant principle has the corrective and final word. But a principle that is not part of the substance inevitably undermines the substance.

The Protestant principle, as we know from sad experience, is so protean and subject to variation that it results either in gutting the tradition or in creating new traditions around which further schisms are formed. Theology that is not in service to "the faith once delivered to the saints" (Jude 3) will, in time, turn against the faith once delivered to the saints. Ideas that are not held accountable to "the Church of the living God, the pillar and bulwark of truth" (I Timothy 3:15) will, in time, become the enemy of that truth. Such was our understanding of the normative claim of the Augsburg Confession to have received nothing contrary to Scripture or the Catholic Church. As would become painfully evident, in an ecclesial community it is not enough that orthodoxy be tolerated as one option among others. Where orthodoxy is optional, it will, in time, be proscribed. The truth of that axiom is today on sad display in the agonies of liberal Protestantism. For a long time, I thought that Lutheranism might be spared.

Spared for what? Spared to fulfill the Reformation intention to be a movement of gospel reform within the one, holy, catholic, and apostolic Church. For many years, I worked for the fulfillment of that intention. While still in my twenties, when I was pastor of a vibrant and mainly African American parish in one of the poorest sections of Brooklyn, I was also editor of *Una Sancta*, an ecumenical journal of theology in the Piepkorn tradition. Later, I edited for sixteen years *Forum Letter*, a rallying center for evangelical catholics, devoting my energies to what I termed "the healing of the breach of the sixteenth century between Rome and the Reformation." For a long time, there seemed to be believable, although painfully slow, movement toward that goal. A hopeful sign in the 1970s was the Lutheran reappropriation of a large part of Catholic liturgical substance in the production of the *Lutheran Book of Worship*. And there were the Lutheran–Roman Catholic theological dialogues that, for a long time, helped sustain the hope that ecclesial reconciliation could be sighted on the distant horizon.

But what was happening within Lutheranism, in America and elsewhere, was not kind to that hope. In this country, the Evangelical Lutheran Church in America (ELCA), an amalgamation of three earlier bodies, was moving into full communion with liberal Protestant churches that, on crucial questions such as the Real Presence, rejected the "catholic substance" to which the Lutheran tradition was presumably pledged. Real existent Lutheranism—as distinct from Lutheranism as a theological idea—had decisively turned against the fulfillment of its vocation as a reforming movement within the one Church. My reluctant and painful conclusion was that Lutheranism had settled into being a permanently separated Protestant denomination, or, as the case may be, several denominations, among many other permanently separated Protestant denominations.

To this day, some of my Lutheran friends say that, in becoming Catholic, I acted precipitously, that I jumped the gun. To which I say that I hope they are right. If someday, in some way that cannot now be foreseen, Lutheranism changes direction and moves toward that healing of the breach of the sixteenth century, I would like to think that my decision may have played a small part in that redirection. There is today no evidence of such a redirection, but there is overwhelming evidence that Lutheranism has decisively abandoned the ecclesial commitment of the Augsburg Confession as that commitment was so hopefully construed by its evangelical catholics.

I had no right to be angry about that, although I sometimes was. After all, Lutheranism is a voluntary association. Its identity, beliefs, and practices are subject to democratic debate and majority vote. Yes, its congregations and clergy were solemnly pledged to the Augsburg Confession, but the meaning of that pledge is accommodated to changing times, and such accommodation is facilitated by the talents of theologians in constructing what they believe to be a new and better Lutheranism. Who was I, and who were we evangelical catholics, to impose our construal of the Church of the Augsburg Confession on everybody else? True, we had considerable, albeit minority, support in the guild of theologians; but, with pitiably few exceptions, the millions of Lutherans who constitute real existent Lutheranism had always thought that theirs was one Protestant denomination among others. They were Germans or Swedes or Danes or Norwegians; and Germans (those who were not Catholic) and Swedes and Danes and Norwegians had always belonged to the Protestant church called Lutheran. Our evangelical catholic notion that Lutheranism is

in exile from the Catholic Church and that there is now no reason to continue to live in exile was alien. Our talk about healing
the breach of the sixteenth century was, for the most part, tolerated as an interesting ecumenical idea, but it had no bearing on
faith, life, and worship at, say, Trinity Lutheran Church in Milwaukee, nor on the agenda of the next national convention or
church-wide assembly.

In the parish of which I was pastor I, like other evangelical
catholic pastors, could cultivate an enclave of catholic faith,
practice, and sensibilities. But it was just that, an enclave.
Within the larger Lutheran reality, such parishes were tolerated
as an eccentricity, but they had no bearing on what
Lutheranism was or intended to be. Within my parish, I was
priest, bishop, and pope, accountable to no Magisterium but my
own. I and similarly situated pastors could in teaching and in
liturgical and sacramental practice become ever more catholic,
but it did not bring us any closer into communion with uppercase Catholicism. And that is because Catholicism is not just
ideas and practices but the apostolically constituted community
that is the Catholic Church. The Catholic Church is as historically specifiable in space and time as is the City of New York.
Other places might be ever so much like New York but, unless
they are in New York, they are not New York. Substitute London, Chicago, or Venice. You are not there unless you are there.
It is not sufficient to cultivate spaces where, with a few others,
you can think, and almost believe, that you are there.

We evangelical catholics insisted that Lutheranism, *authentic*
Lutheranism, was on its way to there. The reality that is
Lutheranism, however, was moving in a different direction.
Evangelical catholicism proposed an *idea* of Lutheranism, but

an idea is not a church. There came a time in the life of John Henry Newman when he was forced to recognize that his insistence on the catholicity of the Church of England had resulted in his creation of "a paper church." His Anglicanism was vibrantly alive in his own head, and he could write about it eloquently, but it was not Anglicanism. He could cite document after document in support of his argument for what the Church of England should be, but wishing did not make it so. The same, I reluctantly concluded, is true of the Church of the Augsburg Confession. I was told that I had an obligation to the cause of evangelical catholicism, that I owed a loyalty to the Lutheranism that might yet be, and I thought long and hard about that. Until it became evident to me that what I called my loyalty was not to Lutheranism but to my idea of Lutheranism, which is to say that it was loyalty to myself, which is no loyalty at all.

The problem went deep. I was in love with my idea, I was loyal to my idea, and I had spent years calling others to a similar love and loyalty. Yet although it was an idea shared, and therefore *our* idea, it was still no more than an idea. An idea such as this is what Newman dismissively referred to as a "theory." A theory, he explained, is "notional" rather than "real." As I said earlier, whoever becomes a Catholic by following an intellectual or theological path, or by following other paths that he cannot help but think about in intellectual or theological ways, finds himself in the company of Newman. And when one inquires deeply into the difference between love for and loyalty to oneself and one's ideas, on the one hand, and love and loyalty ordered to the truth, on the other, one finds oneself in the company of the fifth-century St. Augustine.

Lutheranism understands itself to be Augustinian, and in some ways it is. The root of all sin, said Luther, following Augustine, is a condition described in two words: *Incurvatus est*—we are turned in upon ourselves. The young Augustine, like people of all times, including our own, thought he was searching for God. Yet in his mastery of all the philosophical paths, he was the master, and therein was the problem. Finally, he faced the question: "What am I to myself but a guide to my own self-destruction?" Perhaps his best-known line is this: "You have made us for yourself, O Lord, and our hearts are restless until they rest in you." Rest comes with surrender, with being shaken out of the state of *incurvatus est*, with submission to an other, and finally to the Other. The Other is embodied, as in the body of Christ, the Church. The form of the body, most fully and rightly ordered through time, has a location as specific as the location of New York. *Finitum capax infiniti*—the finite is capable of the infinite. One's search could not forever stop short of the finite that is the Catholic Church.

3 | The Authority in Question

Among the prominent intellectuals and theologians who have in the last few years entered into full communion with the Catholic Church is R. R. Reno, formerly an Anglican. Each of these thinkers would likely explain the decision to become Catholic in a different way, but I expect that most would be sympathetic to the reasons given by Reno. In *First Things*, he wrote: "In order to escape the insanity of my slide into self-guidance, I put myself up for reception into the Catholic Church as one might put oneself up for adoption. A man can no more guide his spiritual life by his ideas than a child can raise himself on the strength of his native potential." Reno quotes Newman, who, while he was still an Anglican, said that "the Church of Rome preoccupies the ground." Reno understands that to mean:

> She is a given, a primary substance within the economy of denominationalism. Thus one could rightly say that I became a Catholic by default, and that possibility is the simple gift I

received from the Catholic Church. She needed neither reasons, nor theories, nor ideas from me.[1]

What stands out is the sheer *isness* of the Catholic Church. To sustain the allegiance of an ecclesial Christian, the Church of the Augsburg Confession needed reasons, theories, and ideas from me and others of like mind. It *was* our idea. To give yourself to your own idea is not to give yourself at all. It is possible that I might make some small contribution to the Catholic Church, also along the line of reasons, theories, and ideas. But the Catholic Church does not need anything from me for it to be the Catholic Church. The Catholic Church is not about me. She is in her isness grandly and blithely indifferent to the tangle that constitutes my state of *incurvatus est*. Like a mother, she takes me in.

To speak of the Church as a mother or to speak, as Reno does, of putting oneself up for adoption raises a field of red flags for those of a Freudian bent. Is this not an instance of letting oneself be infantilized? And Jesus said, "Unless you become as little children . . ." It is not a regression to childhood but a progression beyond adulthood falsely defined as the autonomous self, as the gloriously independent actualization of *me*. It is what the French philosopher Paul Ricoeur describes as "the second naïveté," the rebirth of wonder that had been so long stifled under endless complexifications. It is, on the far side of the notional, to surrender to the real. It is even, I dare to think, to be surprised by the unfamiliar and unexpected experience of something like humility. (A Jewish friend said he would not think of missing my service of ordination: "Just once, I want to see Richard prostrated before somebody.")

The morning after I was received into full communion by Cardinal O'Connor, I woke up and tried to specify just what it was that seemed so different. Then it dawned upon me: For the first time in years I did not begin the day oppressed by the burden of wondering where I was supposed to be and of explaining why I was not there. I was there. The cliché is as banal as it is inevitable: I had come home. I had long resisted the sentimentalized talk about "Rome sweet home." I had cheered when Cardinal Johannes Willebrands, then in charge of the Vatican's office of Christian unity, had declared, "The word 'return' is no longer part of our ecumenical vocabulary." But I knew I had returned; I knew I had come home. More precisely, I knew there was nowhere else to go. And that is something like being home. It was the place that, as a Lutheran, I had left more than four hundred years ago, and now I had returned.

I had no illusions about the problems, confusions, and conflicts within the Catholic Church. As a "separated brother" I had been thinking and speaking and writing about all that for years. I was not sure how my thinking and writing would be received now that it was, so to speak, all in the family. But none of that mattered. There was nowhere else to go. Within a few months of my reception, a Catholic publication put me on its cover as "Catholic of the Year." I suggested to the editors that maybe they should have waited until I had been a Catholic for at least a year.

As it turns out, the reception has been mixed. As a Lutheran, I had over the years received dozens of honorary degrees and awards from Catholic colleges and universities. Making such awards was the ecumenical thing to do. Now that I am in the family, writing and saying much as I did before, the bestowing of such honors is thought to be a controversial thing to do. Were I a prophet, which I am not, one might recall the maxim that a prophet is not without honor unless he gets too close. As it is, I have not one complaint. My welcome has been far beyond my deserving. And, anyway, there is nowhere else to go.

I am frequently asked whether I had ever considered becoming Orthodox. Eastern Orthodoxy is a real alternative for the ecclesial Christian. The churches of the East are recognized as "sister churches" by Rome. Orthodoxy possesses so many of the essentials—apostolic ministry and doctrine, a magnificent richness of liturgy and sacramental life, a powerful theological tradition of humanity's destined end in the life of God, a fervent devotion to Mary and the saints. One does have to consider Orthodoxy. But I am a Western Christian, with all that it entails: Augustine and Thomas Aquinas on nature and grace, reason and revelation, sin and forgiveness; as well as the Reformation refractions of those great themes and the continuing disputes they have occasioned. Moreover, Orthodoxy is powerfully shaped by ethnic and national identities—Russian, Greek, Romanian, Armenian—to which I am a stranger.

The late Father Alexander Schmemann, a dear friend, was long-time dean of St. Vladimir Theological Seminary in New York. He spoke often of converts, mainly Lutherans and Anglicans, who posed great difficulties to themselves and to the Orthodox Church by their attempts to become what, by virtue of their life histories, they were not. Much more important, becoming Orthodox does nothing to remedy the problem of not being in communion with the Petrine Ministry exercised by the bishop of Rome. Becoming Orthodox would do nothing to advance a lifelong commitment to healing the sixteenth-century breach between Rome and the Reformation. Some might ask whether my becoming Catholic advances that healing, a fair question to which I hope the answer is in the affirmative. My becoming Catholic is at least a testimony to that commitment and a personal anticipation of its fulfillment.

But one cannot leave the question of the Orthodox option without acknowledging the great sadness of continuing division between East and West. In view of all that is shared between Catholic and Orthodox, it seems fair to say that the only thing missing for full communion is full communion. One day in a discussion with John Paul II, I asked him what were his greatest hopes for his pontificate when he was elected in 1978. Without a moment's hesitation he said that his greatest hope was for Christian unity. And Christian unity means, first of all, reconciliation with the Orthodox Church. John Paul repeatedly spoke of the need for the Church "to breathe again with both lungs, East and West." Despite John Paul's many conciliatory initiatives, that hope has been delayed, but his pontificate laid the groundwork for the healing of the thousand-year breach between East and West. That is a great achievement, and I have no doubt that it is an achievement on which Benedict XVI will build.

Already in the early months of the new pontificate, the Russian Church, which has been among the chief obstacles to rapprochement, seems to be more responsive to initiatives from Rome. History has many ironies in the fire, as it is said, and it may be that the Russians are less uneasy dealing with a German than with a Pole, given the long and bitter history of intra-Slavic conflict.

In becoming a Catholic, one is braced for certain criticisms. Among the most common, usually coming from Protestant sources, is that the person who becomes a Catholic has a "felt need for authority." This is usually said in a somewhat condescending manner by people who say they are able to live with the ambiguities and tensions that some of us cannot handle. But to say that I have a felt need for authority is no criticism at all. Of course I have, as should we all. The allegedly autonomous self who acknowledges no authority but himself is abjectly captive to the authority of a tradition of Enlightenment rationality that finally collapses into incoherence. Whether in matters of science, history, religion, or anything else of consequence, we live amid a storm of different and conflicting ideas claiming to be the truth. Confronted by such truth claims, we necessarily ask, "Sez who?" By what authority, by whose authority, should I credit such claims to truth? Answering the question requires a capacity to distinguish between the authoritative and the authoritarian.

All Christians believe that God has revealed himself in the history of Israel and in the culmination of that history, Jesus Christ, who is the Word of God. All believe, further, that this revelation is authoritatively interpreted by the witness of the apostles, and that over the first centuries this witness was collected and "canonized" by continuing apostolic authority in what came to be called the New Testament, which is the written Word of God. The question is not about the "felt need for authority" but about where that authority is located and how it is exercised. This touches on a familiar dispute between Protestants and Catholics that has been ongoing since the sixteenth century. The dispute is usually framed as the authority of the

Bible vs. the authority of the Church, or the authority of the Bible vs. the authority of "tradition." But that way of framing the question is, I believe, deeply incoherent.

The Protestant and Catholic positions are rival traditions in conflict. The promise of Jesus that he would send the Holy Spirit to guide his disciples into all truth is a promise made to the Church. That promise is fulfilled, in part, in the gift of the Spirit-inspired writings of the New Testament. But the guidance of the Spirit did not end there. The promise is that the Spirit would guide the Church until the end of time. The Spirit guided the Church in the writing of the inspired texts; guided the Church in recognizing which texts, of the many claiming inspiration at the time, were truly inspired; guided the Church in determining what would be the canon of the New Testament; and guided the Church in declaring the unique authority of the canonical texts for all time. In sum, it is the Spirit guiding the Church from beginning to end, and the end is not yet.

In this understanding, what is crucial is the apostolic foundation and continuing apostolic character of the Church. We Christians confess in the Nicene Creed that we believe in "one, holy, catholic, and apostolic Church"—not in one, holy, catholic, and *biblical* Church. Under the guidance of the Holy Spirit, the Bible is entirely the book of, by, and for the Church, and should never be pitted against the Church. In reaction to the sixteenth-century Protestant rejection of tradition as authoritative, Catholics affirmed a "two sources" theory of revealed truth—the Bible *and* tradition. That way of putting the matter gave rise to numerous misunderstandings, and the formulation was further developed and refined at the Second Vatican Council in the Constitution on Revelation, *Dei Verbum* (The Word of God).

In a statement of 2002, participants in the ecumenical theological project called Evangelicals and Catholics Together were able to say:

Together we affirm that Scripture is the divinely inspired and uniquely authoritative written revelation of God; as such it is normative for the teaching and life of the Church. We also affirm that tradition, rightly understood as the proper reflection of biblical teaching, is the faithful transmission of the truth of the gospel from generation to generation through the power of the Holy Spirit. As Evangelicals and Catholics fully committed to our respective heritages, we affirm together the coinherence of Scripture and tradition: Tradition is not a second source of revelation alongside the Bible but must ever be corrected and informed by it, and Scripture itself is not understood in a vacuum apart from the historical existence and life of the community of faith.

"The historical existence and life of the community of faith" is another way of saying tradition. Again, a fair-minded reading of the New Testament leaves no doubt that Jesus intended a continuing community of discipleship that is the Church. There is also no doubt that he commissioned the apostles to shepherd that community under the guidance of the Holy Spirit. From the beginning, disputes arose over faith and morals. In the New Testament and in the patristic literature of the first centuries, it is clear that such disputes were to be resolved by appeal to the authority of the apostles and apostolic churches. Later, the appeal was to bishops in council, the bishops being recognized as successors to the apostles. (In the

Catholic counting, as noted earlier, Nicea in 325 was the first council and Vatican II was the twenty-first. An argument can be made that the first council, or at least the first exercise of the conciliar principle, is to be found in the fifteenth chapter of Acts when the apostles addressed the question of what was to be required of non-Jewish believers.) Admittedly, it is a long and complicated path from the New Testament to Nicea and on to today's exercise of the Magisterium in the Catholic Church, but, in logic and in form, the story is one of clear continuity. It is the story of the apostles gathered by and around Peter.

The division between East and West means that not all the successors to the apostles are gathered, and then there are the millions of Christians in non-apostolically ordered communities who are not part of the deliberation. John Paul II spoke of what might be done about these imperfections in his 1995 encyclical *Ut Unum Sint* (That They May be One). Yet, in this state of Christianity divided, the Catholic Church makes a uniquely believable claim to having maintained the form and logic from the beginning. That, too, is entailed in saying that she is the Church of Jesus Christ most fully and rightly ordered through time.

When as a young man I was first in Rome, I was Protestant enough to be inured to much of the splendor and the glory. Was the magnificence of Michelangelo's basilica of St. Peter, I asked myself, worth the scandal of the sale of indulgences that paid for it and helped precipitate the schisms of the sixteenth century? Midst Rome's aesthetic effusion of Catholic substance, I kept a firm hold on Protestant principle. Until one afternoon, I remember it now quite clearly, I was struck by the fact that Peter and Paul, the two chief pillars of the apostolic community, both

ended up in Rome and there they were crowned with martyrdom. I was already aware of that, of course, but then I
recognized the ecclesial logic and form; the rightness of it, the
necessity of it.

So what? one may ask. It is a contingent fact, it might have
been otherwise. But the whole of Christianity is composed of
contingent facts. In the abstract, everything might have been
otherwise, but it was not and is not. It is this and that, and thus
and so. Abraham, a burning bush, Sinai, exile, mysterious
prophecies, a virgin conceiving, water into wine, a cross, a
death, his appearance to share a meal of fish (after they had
caught exactly 153 of them!), Corinthians speaking in tongues,
Peter and Paul in Rome, Constantine and an empire won and
lost, Benedict and the monastic anticipation of the new
Jerusalem, a papacy divided and a papacy healed, Francis Xavier
and the gospel carried to the ends of the earth, and along the
way the greatest of minds and souls—Irenaeus and the Gre-
gories and Augustine and Anselm and Catherine and Teresa and
Thomas Aquinas and von Balthasar and John Paul II—provide
the narrative, stating and restating what it all means. It could
have been otherwise, but it wasn't, and it isn't. It is all contingent, which is to say it is all history, the history of a distinct
people. And that afternoon, as I contemplated Peter and Paul in
Rome, I knew that I had to be, and had to be indisputably, part
of that people that was and is the Catholic Church. Sooner or
later, I think I knew then, I would have to put myself up for
adoption into that people.

Upon becoming a Catholic and then a Catholic priest, I
made a solemn profession of faith that included these words:
"With firm faith, I also believe everything contained in the

Word of God, whether written or handed down in Tradition, which the Church, either by a solemn judgement or by the ordinary and universal Magisterium, sets forth to be believed as divinely revealed." I took a deep breath before saying those words. Am I writing a blank check on my soul? What if the Magisterium, the solemn teaching office of the Church, gets something wrong? May I even admit that question to my mind? By what criterion, by what measure, could I judge a teaching to be wrong? Newman raged against the ravages of "private judgment." Is private the same as personal? Or am I making an intensely personal judgment to believe what the Church believes? Martin Luther spoke derisively of what he called the coal miner's faith. Asked what he believed, the coal miner answered, "I believe what the Church believes." Asked what the Church believes, he answered, "The Church believes what I believe." Luther insisted that that is no faith at all. I am not quite so sure.

I mentioned earlier the act of faith. For the Protestant, the act of faith is an act of faith in Christ, and only then, if at all, is it an act of faith in the Church. They are two acts of faith. For the Catholic, the act of faith in Christ and his Church is one act of faith. In the Nicene Creed we do not say, "I believe *that there is* one, holy, catholic, and apostolic Church." We say, "I believe *in* one holy, catholic, and apostolic Church." Because I believe in Christ, I believe in his Church, I entrust myself to her. Christ the head and the Church his body constitute the *totus Christus*, the total Christ. However it may be that the Church is present in other communities, there is no other community that is prepared to, that would dare to, that should dare to, accept my unqualified trust. I once read an interview with a writer whose name I now forget. He was asked why he went to Mass. "Because I do not know what else I would do with my gratitude," he answered. I am a Catholic because, among many other reasons, I do not know what else I would do with my trust. Trust is risk, trust is faith. Not blind faith but faith with eyes wide open. Christ as true God and true man can, by definition, not betray my trust. But the troubling thought is not easily dismissed: The *totus Christus*, including his very human Church, conceivably could betray my trust. I believe she never will.

But how can I *know* that? How can I know so much that I believe to be true except by believing it to be true? Trust, which is an act of love, is a way of knowing. How can a bride know that the bridegroom will be faithful? Or vice versa? The image is apt, for we are told that the Church is the bride of Christ, and it is no secret that the people who are the Church have, like Israel of old, often gone a-whoring. But also like Israel of old, she is still the people of God. Through Scripture, councils, and the Magisterium she has taught truly, although her children, in positions high and low, have not always been faithful to her teaching. There is development of doctrine, clarification of doctrine, refinement of doctrine, and there will be until the end of time. But there is neither change nor contradiction of doctrine. Where others claim to see change or contradiction, I see development and refinement with a vision transformed by love. I, too, can construe such development as change and contradiction. It is easy to do. I choose to view it as Spirit-guided development and refinement. I accept responsibility for that choice. The apostolic leadership of the Church has been given the authority to judge. I choose to obey.

Ah, now we come to the crunch point: obedience. Nothing is more alien, nothing more offensive, to the autonomous self who judges all and is judged by none. Obedience speaks of a love that obliges, as all love does oblige. From the Latin *obedire*, obedience means to give ear to, to listen responsively. The gift of reason is ordered to truth, and truth commands obedience. Yes, but what if . . . There are so many *what ifs*. The obstacles on the way to becoming Catholic are typically posed as *what if*. For instance, the Church claims, under certain carefully specified conditions, to teach infallibly. The dogma of infallibility was defined by the First Vatican Council in 1870 and has given rise to many misunderstandings. It means, quite simply, that the Church will never invoke her full authority to require anyone to believe what is false. The Church also teaches infallibly that nothing that she teaches infallibly about faith and morals is incompatible with God's good gift of reason. Yes, but *what if* she did at some time in the future? For instance, *what if* a pope, invoking the fullness of infallible authority, declared that Mary is, along with Father, Son, and Holy Spirit, the fourth person in the Godhead? What if, indeed.

Once again, to think with the Church *(sentire cum ecclesia)* begins with thinking. *If* a pope were to say that he is infallibly declaring that God is the Holy Quaternity rather than the Holy Trinity, it would pose much the same problem as a pope's declaring that 2+2=5. Under the direction of the Magisterium, the Church can develop and refine doctrine, but she cannot teach anything that contradicts the core truths of the tradition (the "deposit of faith") or that cannot reasonably be believed. Were a pope to say that Mary is God or that 2+2=5, a loving and faithful response might be to say that one has misheard or misunderstood what was said. One might pray that the pope will clarify his statement, or be replaced by a pope who does not cause such confusion. Certainly I would not be bound to believe that Mary is God or that 2+2=5. But this way of thinking is fundamentally wrongheaded. To be obsessed with *what ifs* is to remain captive to fear. The apostle John tells us that "perfect love casts out fear." One finally makes a decision based either on fear and suspicion or on love and trust. It is true that by taking the first way one may avoid a great error; but, if the decision is wrong, one has suffered the loss of an immeasurably greater good. With respect to the big decisions of life, we each choose our own form of risk. Modern agnosticism assumes that our desires are an obstacle to finding the truth. But our desires may also be a guide to truth: They may lead us to the discovery that what we desire is the truth.

Many things are conceivable in the abstract, also things that are contrary to fact. Ask a faithful and loving husband and wife what they would do or think if the other was having an affair on the side. In the abstract, it is conceivable, but what is the point? It is at best a thought experiment, and a marriage is not a thought experiment. So also the Church and one's adherence to her teaching authority is not a thought experiment. It is a living relationship of trust. There may at times be difficulties. But one remembers Newman's maxim: Ten thousand difficulties do not add up to a doubt. In this context, a doubt means a decision not to believe. The Church has not invoked and will not invoke her full authority to require anyone to believe what is false. That is a judgment of reason based upon experience. It is also a statement of faith, as in the solemnly undertaken "Profession of Faith."

There is another dimension of magisterial authority that sometimes occasions considerable confusion. I only touch on it here because it will enter the story later. That dimension is "the sense of the faithful," known as the *sensus fidelium*. Newman made much of the claim that in the fourth century most of the bishops subscribed to the Arian heresy, the belief that the Son is not co-equally God with the Father. It was the faith of the ordinary believers, the *sensus fidelium*, that preserved the orthodox truth that was later and definitively affirmed by the bishops in council. On certain controverted questions today, some Catholics who describe themselves as progressive appeal to the *sensus fidelium* against the Magisterium. Issues commonly agitated are democracy in the Church, priestly celibacy, the ordination of women, homosexuality, contraception, in vitro fertilization, and, much less commonly, the prohibition of abortion.

A brief word on each is in order to clarify our thinking about the *sensus fidelium*. The issues will crop up again in other connections. It is commonly said the Church is not a democracy, and that is true, although not sufficient. Political democracy is constituted by the idea of the sovereign will of the people. The Church is constituted by the sovereign will of Christ. It is a matter of doctrine that the responsibility for the leadership of the Church rests with her ordained ministers under the apostolic authority of the bishop exercised "with and under" the bishop of Rome. In a democratic ethos such as ours, however, it is the better part of wisdom for bishops to exercise their authority within a context of accountability and participation that instills confidence in their leadership. (The failure to do that, incidentally, had a great deal to do with the furor of the sex abuse scandals that erupted in January 2002.)

The requirement that priests be celibate is, it is said, a matter not of doctrine but of discipline, and it could be changed tomorrow. That, too, is true but not sufficient. The celibacy rule is grounded in and formed by a doctrine and spirituality of priesthood that goes back to Christian beginnings. There are a few married priests, mainly married Lutheran and Episcopal clergy who became Catholics. Were the general rule of celibacy abandoned, it might well, as advocates contend, result in an increase of priestly vocations. (Although I know manly young men whose attraction to the radical vocation of priesthood is, they say, enhanced by the sacrifice involved in celibacy.) Dropping the rule would also bring foreseen and unforeseen consequences for the financial support of clergy, the perception of priests who choose not to marry, and the prospect of marital problems and divorce among priests who do marry. In any event, the ancient tradition of a celibate priesthood—which, contra those who agitate for change, goes back far before the late Middle Ages—has been strongly supported by modern popes and is likely to endure.

The *sensus fidelium* was invoked also for the ordination of women to the priesthood. Apart from a few Gnostic sects in the early centuries, Christianity had never had female priests (or, perhaps more accurately, priestesses). But then, with the feminist surge in the 1970s, Episcopalians, followed by the Church of England, began ordaining women; many thought it only a matter of time before the Catholic Church did the same. Today, the once vigorous agitation for female priests has largely dissipated. The pope solemnly declared that the Church is "not authorized" to ordain women and therefore cannot do it. The Congregation for the Doctrine of the Faith (CDF) has said that that declaration is infallible. Some hardcore progressives have argued that the CDF is itself not infallible and therefore cannot infallibly say whether or not a papal declaration is infallible. It is a nice debating point, but it is almost impossible to envision how the settled doctrine could be unsettled in the future.

Even if there were a possible doubt about whether women could be priests, the Church could not ordain in doubt without throwing the entire sacramental order into question. The theo-logic is unassailable: A validly ordained minister is essential for a valid Eucharist and the sacramental forgiveness of sins. Dubious ministry means dubious sacraments. Female priests would, in time, mean female bishops doubtfully ordaining other priests, with the result that the entire sacramental life of the Church would be riddled through and through with uncertainty. If one were not convinced by magisterial declarations and the argument from doubt, there is an additional consideration: Ordaining women would shatter all hopes of reconciliation with the East because, if one can say never about anything in history, the Orthodox will never ordain women, and reconciliation is impossible without the mutual recognition of ministries. Finally, the Church is universal, but agitation for women's ordination was almost exclusively located in North America and a highly secularized Western Europe. In the Southern Hemisphere, where Catholicism and other Christian movements are growing most rapidly, there is almost no sympathy for such a change, and there is powerful opposition against it.

In progressive Catholic circles in this country, the ordination of women had for a couple of decades an air of inevitability about it. It was only a question of time. In support of the claim that the *sensus fidelium* had been heard from, polls were produced showing that a large majority of Catholics in the United

States favored ordaining women. In fact, polls on this question, as well as the question of married priests, showed that, *if* the Church were to change her practice, most Catholics would favor the change. Few were *demanding* change. The move for women's ordination is an important case study in the exercise of the Church's teaching authority. For the proponents of the change, it is but another sign of the hopeless recalcitrance of a reactionary Church. For others, it is reassuring evidence of the Church's integrity under powerful pressures of cultural conformity. And, of course, the pressures to conform are not only surrounding the Church but also very much within the Church.

The *sensus fidelium* is not so frequently invoked in the instance of homosexuality, perhaps because the great majority of Americans, Catholic and non-Catholic, essentially agree with the Church's teaching. The teaching is that homosexual acts are "intrinsically disordered," and those who experience homosexual desires are to be lovingly supported in striving to live chaste lives. The Church urges firm resistance to the grim doctrine that homosexuality is simply a matter of fate, and to the dehumanizing idea that one's core identity is determined by one's sexual desires. We are more, immeasurably more, than our sexual desires. And morally disordered desires are hardly limited to homosexuality, or to sexual desires of any kind. Those who succumb to homosexual desires are, like all sinners, to be loved and assured of the transforming power of God's forgiveness. In law and social practice, they should not be subjected to unjust discrimination, but neither should the practices that define "the gay community" be put on a social or moral par with the union of man and woman in marriage. In sum, the Church's teaching is pretty much the popular intuitive wisdom about the right ordering of human sexuality.

Here, too, the appeal is to "natural law." The Church's teaching, one may confidently say, will not change, and the popular wisdom is not likely to change, despite relentless advocacy to the contrary. We will return later to the question of homosexuality, for it is very much part of the sex abuse scandals that have wracked the Church in this country.

The appeal to the *sensus fidelium* against the teaching authority of the Magisterium is most pronounced on the question of artificial contraception. Herein lies a long and dismal tale of what must be acknowledged as a failure of leadership. In 1968, after several years of apparent uncertainty in which it seemed the question of contraception, and of "the pill" in particular, was up for grabs, Pope Paul VI issued the encyclical *Humanae Vitae*; in it, he affirmed the traditional teaching that sexual intercourse and openness to new life are morally inseparable. This had been the historic teaching of the Church, and many observers have argued that the great mistake of Paul VI was in appearing to hesitate before reaffirming it. Defenders of *Humanae Vitae* persuasively argue that it was in many ways a prophetic document that accurately foretold what would happen once sex and procreation are separated. What Paul VI said would happen has happened. When sex asserts its own rights to pleasure and the satisfaction of needs, pleasure and satisfaction are divorced from responsibility, the bond of marriage is loosened, promiscuity is made easier, disordered forms of sexual expression are declared normal, and unintended new life is deemed expendable. Those who contend that there is a logical continuum from artificial contraception to abortion are right, I believe, but they are probably in a distinct minority among Catholics today.

In America and throughout the developed world, Catholics practice artificial contraception at about the same rate as the general population. How did this happen? In the years before 1968 and *Humanae Vitae*, while Paul VI appeared to hesitate, progressive theologians confidently predicted that the "outdated" teaching on contraception would be modified or abrogated. This expectation was widely disseminated through the media. On the chance that Paul VI would reaffirm the traditional teaching, and in advance of his issuing *Humanae Vitae*, some theologians organized a coordinated public rejection of the encyclical. A few bishops, acting in the belief that they are responsible for guarding the Church's teaching, attempted to discipline the dissenting theologians; but they backed off when faced with a firestorm of negative media reaction and, more important, Rome's fear that confrontation might lead to a schism in the Church in the United States. I admit that this is too brief an account of one of the most complex and consequential moments in the history of Catholicism in America.

The result, almost four decades later, is that most Catholics, if they are even aware that the Church once prohibited artificial contraception, assume that the teaching has been effectively nullified. The great majority of Catholics, it is fair to say, have never heard the teaching set forth from the pulpit, and they would be quite taken aback by a homily setting forth what, in fact, the Church teaches. But, it is objected, that is to miss the point. The point is that the *sensus fidelium* participates in the teaching authority of the Church, and, if popular belief and practice reject what is officially taught, then what is officially taught is not authentic Catholic teaching. Well, not quite. On second thought, not at all. The appeal to the *sensus fidelium* depends on what the Church teaches about the *sensus fidelium*. And here is what the Second Vatican Council teaches: "The whole body of the faithful . . . cannot err in matters of belief. This characteristic is shown in the supernatural appreciation of faith *(sensus fidei)* on the part of the whole people, when 'from the bishops to the last of the faithful,' they manifest a universal consent in matters of faith and morals." (*Lumen Gentium* 12, with a quote from St. Augustine.)

There is something like a Catch–22 here. If the sense of the faithful (or the supernatural sense of faith—*sensus fidei*) is measured by the belief of those who are faithful, then those who are not faithful to the Church's teaching do not have a voice in defining what is the Church's teaching. One may be forgiven for suspecting an element of circularity in this reasoning. Those who disagree with the official Magisterium are, by definition, not faithful and therefore are not part of the *sensus fidelium* that bears witness to the truth of what the Magisterium teaches. In untangling this knotty question, it may be useful to recall Newman's example of how the faithful held out for what would come to be recognized as orthodoxy when most of the bishops were leaning toward the Arian heresy. In the liturgy and devotional life of the Church, the faithful intuited the necessity of affirming that Jesus Christ is at once true God and true man. They knew they *worshiped* Jesus Christ as God and, if he were not God, they would be guilty of idolatry. The bishops assembled in council would in time be led by the Spirit to recognize and ratify what the faithful believed.

Is that comparable, as some progressive Catholics claim, to what is happening today with respect to contraception, in vitro fertilization, and other questions related to human sexuality? I think not. True, there are some Catholic theologians and ethicists who contend that artificial contraception, for instance, is in harmony with Catholic faith, but almost without exception these are writers who challenge the teaching authority of the Magisterium as such, and not just on contraception. They belong to the academic theological guild that orchestrated the rejection of *Humanae Vitae* when it appeared and that proposes itself as a "parallel magisterium" to that of the bishops in union with the pope. They frequently claim the support of the *sensus fidelium*, but there is little or no evidence that the many Catholics who contravene church teaching on contraception or in vitro fertilization think that they are bearing witness to a more authentic Catholic teaching. Some who are aware of the Church's teaching feel guilty about what they are doing. Many are unaware of the teaching or have never had it presented to them in a manner intended to be persuasive. Almost all have received the impression, communicated explicitly or by silence, that contravening whatever may be the Church's teaching is no big deal. Anecdotal evidence suggests that in the confessional few Catholics confess the use of artificial contraception, and probably a minority of priests tell them that they should. The widespread ignorance or indifference of Catholics on these questions is not an instance in which the *sensus fidelium* is trying to inform the mind of the Church; it is, rather, a moral debacle resulting from a massive failure of pastoral leadership—particularly the failure of bishops—to help the faithful to think with the Church, as in *sentire cum ecclesia*.

Nonetheless, there is and will likely always be a relatively small group of Catholic activists who will continue to agitate for changing the Church's teaching and practice on all the above-mentioned questions. Often, well-meaning people do believe that the *sensus fidelium* mandates something like the democratizing of the Church. There is today, for instance, The Voice of the Faithful, and an older group going back to the 1970s, Call to Action. Groups such as these receive media attention because they fit the decades-long story line that has Catholicism in internal turmoil and crisis and the little people rebelling against an authoritarian hierarchy. There is turmoil, and even crisis, as we shall see, but it is usually not along the lines being pressed by these advocacy groups.

A few years ago, Call to Action announced that it was embarking on a one-year drive to get a million signatures in support of the changes we have been discussing. In this "mobilization," all stops were pulled in the network of leftward Catholic publications and organizations. At the end of the year, the organizers announced they would need another year to reach their goal. It was pointed out by some that 1 million signatures from a community of 65 million Catholics fell somewhat short of a credible expression of the voice of the faithful. As it happened, the organizers ended up with about 34,000 signatures, which is 0.0005 percent of the Catholics in the country and about 0.0015 percent of regular Mass-goers.

This does not necessarily discredit the causes advocated. After all, sometimes a small minority gets some things right. And no doubt many Catholics are simply indifferent, not caring one way or another about the causes being agitated. But the limp response to the progressive mobilization does discredit the perennially touted notion that there is a major insurrection in the Catholic ranks, portending a revolution in the Church's teaching and governance. In the forty years since

Vatican Council II, the progressive networks promoting their interpretation of the Council have not been able to enlist the active support of more than 40,000 Catholics, and their organizations are largely composed of aging refugees from the "post–Vatican II" revolution that was not to be.

That is not to say that their efforts have been without effect. Despite the populist and anticlerical rhetoric, the effective influence of such organizations is mainly through thousands of progressive priests and nuns who have over the years understood themselves to be the prophets of the "post–Vatican II Church." In the schools and colleges, and in the chancery offices of dioceses, they have a powerful, though now declining, voice. Because they have the time for it, because matters ecclesiastical constitute their primary, if not exclusive, world of engagement, and because they mutually certify one another as experts on a mutually reinforced understanding of "renewal," theirs is a voice heeded by bishops who are, in many cases, in agreement with them. This is not a conspiracy, although some traditionalists claim it is. Unless one wants to get pedantic about it and point out that conspire, from *conspirare*, means to breath together, which they often do. They certainly tend to think together. It is perhaps best described as an instance of what sociologists call "elective affinity." Like attracts and encourages like. It has little or nothing to do with the much-invoked *sensus fidelium*.

The very idea of authority, and of membership in a community constituted by authority, is deeply offensive to what is generally thought to be the American spirit. Autonomy, independence, individualism—such are the marks of Americanism. There is a long and understandable tradition of viewing

Catholicism as un-American. A hundred years ago, in his classic *The Varieties of Religious Experience*, William James defined religion as "the feelings, acts and experiences of individual men in their solitude, so far as they apprehend themselves to stand in relation to whatever they may consider the divine." James, great man though he was, made no secret of his contempt for Catholicism. More recently, the literary critic Harold Bloom argued in *The American Religion* that the natural religion of almost all Americans, no matter what their religious affiliation, is gnosticism. In the tradition of Ralph Waldo Emerson, they deem themselves possessed of a "divine spark" by which spiritual truth is discerned by its agreement with their individual aspiration toward the transcendent. Even a brief visit to the sprawling "spirituality" section of your local Borders or Barnes & Noble will confirm the perduring power of what James and Bloom described as the religious culture of America. This is yet another reason why Catholics need to be less concerned about being "American Catholics" than about being "Catholic Americans." Note that the adjective tends to control the noun. I will return to the significance of that later.

Yves Congar was a French Dominican whose thought had a powerful influence on the way the Second Vatican Council addressed the question of Church and authority. "In its different forms," Congar wrote,

> *tradition is like the conscience of a community or the principle of identity that links one generation with another; it enables them to remain . . . the same people as they go forward throughout history, which transforms all things. . . . Tradition is memory, and memory enriches experience. If we*

remembered nothing it would be impossible to advance; the same would be true if we were bound to a slavish imitation of the past. True tradition is not servility but fidelity.[2]

And that explains, in large part, why so many people, wearied of the sophisticated but delusory intellectual games of the autonomous self, have put themselves up for adoption by the Catholic Church.

4 | Where the Sweet Birds Sang

The great sadness of the pastoral debacle surrounding *Humanae Vitae* is not only that it precipitated a most un-Catholic insurrection against authority but that millions of Catholics have been deprived of the richness of the Church's teaching on human sexuality, love, fidelity, marriage, and the adventure of living fully the culture of life. Those who orchestrated the opposition to *Humanae Vitae* and assured Catholics that it could be ignored with impunity portrayed the encyclical as an essentially negative and legalistic condemnation of artificial contraception. It was in fact a constructive and comprehensive treatment of human sexuality and, as its title suggests, of "human life." Yet there was in its tone enough of the negative and legalistic to play into the hands of those who were determined to nullify its influence.

John Paul II tried to remedy this by setting forth in a winsomely invitational manner the "theology of the body." Today, thousands of young couples have warmly embraced this vision of sexuality as "the mutual gift of self," and along with it, the practice of Natural Family Planning. They express their grateful delight in the discovery that NFP, as it is called, is safer and more effective than artificial means of contraception, and also enhances mutual respect between husband and wife. NFP is not to be confused with the older "rhythm method," which some derisively called "Catholic roulette." Although there is a rapidly growing interest in the theology of the body, the great majority of Catholics have yet to hear about it. It will likely take a generation, or two or three, to remedy the damage done by the attack on *Humanae Vitae* by those who, accusing the Church of being obsessed with sex, delivered millions of Catholics to the tender mercies of a culture kept in perpetual commotion by disordered sexual desire. Along the way, of course, popular confidence in the teaching authority of the Church has been gravely undermined.

There is, however, neither right nor reason to despair. The cliché that the Church thinks in terms of centuries is a cliché because so many have been impressed by the truth of it. In the decades since Vatican II, progressive priests and nuns claiming the authority of the *sensus fidelium* have agitated for changes ranging from the revolutionary to the silly, a good many of the latter being imposed upon long-suffering parishioners, notably in liturgy, music, and catechesis. Traditionalists have gritted their teeth or organized occasional petitions to the bishop, but there has been nothing in this country comparable to France's Archbishop Marcel Lefebvre (1905–1991), who formed the Society of St. Pius X and went into schism with thousands of followers. After years of patient negotiation by Rome, Lefebvre and his movement were finally excommunicated for ordaining bishops on their own and thus compromising the apostolic integrity of the Church's ministry. That has not happened in the United States.

What has happened here supplies ample material for a long and doleful litany of disarray and decline. The major orders of women religious that have disappeared or are rapidly disappearing are the most dramatic examples, and many orders of men are not far behind. Convents and monasteries have been abandoned or turned into nursing homes for aging religious, posing the question of who will be left to turn out the lights. And a question that makes some bishops uneasy: Who will benefit from the sale of properties worth many millions? The number of parochial schools declined sharply, and many of the two-hundred-plus Catholic colleges and universities have preserved but a patina of the Catholic commitment that inspired their beginnings. And there has been a precipitous decline in vocations to the priesthood, which has fueled the agitation for married priests and the ordination of women. On the other hand, in recent years new orders of religious, male and female, have been established and are attracting eager young recruits. After the loss of tens of thousands of teaching nuns, their replacement by lay teachers and administrators in parochial schools must be counted as a success story. And today many more colleges are trying—or talking about trying—to reassert their "Catholic identity." The decline in priestly vocations is bottoming out, and younger priests and seminarians generally evidence the high-spirited resolve that comes with having chosen the road less traveled.

At every point of renewed growth and confidence one encounters bishops, priests, sisters, and lay people who think of themselves as "John Paul II Catholics." Not surprisingly, they warmly welcomed the election of Benedict XVI. After a long winter of discontent and distraction, they discern a "springtime" on the way, and perhaps already here. But the sometimes mindless innovations and reckless experiments of the decades following the Council have taken a severe toll. Some point out that throughout the history of the Church such confusions and dislocations have been normal after a reforming council, a good reason, others think, for not having another council any time soon. Between Trent and Vatican I was three hundred years, and between Vatican I and Vatican II almost a hundred years. Progressives tend to be eager for Vatican III so that the work of Vatican II can be "completed," and many of them are already living in anticipatory obedience to what they are sure its mandates will be. Traditionalists, on the other hand, shudder at the prospect of another council. In this view, at least a century will be needed to heal, if possible, the de facto schism in the Church and restore what Shakespeare, surveying the devastation wrought by Henry VIII, called the bare ruined choirs. Sonnet 73, it is suggested, well describes the state of the Church:

> *That time of year thou may'st in me behold*
> *When yellow leaves, or none, or few, do hang*
> *Upon those boughs which shake against the cold,*
> *Bare ruin'd choirs where late the sweet birds sang.*

Amid such conflicting assessments of this Catholic moment, the form of the Church is recognizably what it has always been. Everything bizarre and brilliant, elevated and debased, is amply represented in a community of more than a billion people tenuously held together—tenuously, at least from our human per-spective—by some four thousand bishops in communion with the bishop of Rome. At a deeper level the whole thing is held together by the Mass, which is to say Christ in the Mass. The disputes that have most conflicted the Church in North America and Western Europe are already being sidelined by the explosive growth of Catholicism, and of the Christian movement more generally, in the Southern Hemisphere. Sixty-five million Americans are but a little more than 5 percent of the Catholics in the world, although, being American, our influence is disproportionate, but not nearly so disproportionate as we may hope or fear. Increasing globalization makes more important, not less important, the Petrine Ministry and its teaching authority. The Petrine Ministry keeps in conversation and, when necessary, keeps in check the many parts of the whole that is the Catholic Church.

In becoming Catholic, one vows obedience to the Church's teaching authority; one promises to listen responsively. The word commonly used in church documents is "docility," but in English that word goes against the grain. To say someone is docile is to suggest that he is tractable and easily led. But perhaps we should use the word precisely because it does go against the grain. This is especially important for theologians, and particularly theologians who think they are, and sometimes are, very clever. We are so good at coming up with "paper churches" of our own construction, and subject to our deconstruction. The real Church is a maddening hodgepodge in which so many things are believed and taught, but within which the charism of the Magisterium is to guard the deposit of faith, the rule of faith, the structure of faith—call it what you will. It is easier to be docile, of course, when the Magisterium is guided by such stellar theological minds as John Paul II and Benedict XVI. The Church has not always been so fortunate, and will not always be so fortunate in the future. One is obedient to the magisterial office, sometimes despite those holding the office. With respect to some bishops, one wishes it were not so necessary to draw so sharp a distinction between the person and the office.

Even a cursory knowledge of Catholic history braces one for the possibility of bad popes and bad bishops who are either ignorant or corrupt, or both. For many of these, don't even ask about holiness. But whoever holds the magisterial office has little room for innovation, and that is a very good thing. The apostolic tradition through Scripture, the councils, and the history of magisterial teaching is specific and not easily modified. It is much tighter, for instance, than the rule of *stare decisis*—the rule to stand by prior decisions—in the decisions of our Supreme Court. The Court can and does reverse itself, even on questions long thought to be settled. The Magisterium of the Church cannot do that on matters of faith and morals that are integral to the deposit of faith. As mentioned earlier, there are those who delight in rummaging through the history of the Church in the hope of discovering instances of alleged changes or contradictions in her teaching. A recent little book by a nun pressing for women's ordination claims to find no less than 172 such instances. They include the rule that women cover their heads in church, the condemnation of usury, the defense of the papal states in the nineteenth century, abstinence from meat on Friday, and on and on. None of these instances offends against the deposit of faith, none is a matter of faith and morals on which the Church has taught in a way that is "irreformable," which means irreversible.[1]

One must admit that in some instances it may be a close call. In the long and tumultuous history of the Church, one can find examples that might be described as change rather than development, as contradiction rather than clarification. I do not think that is true of any matter of faith and morals on which the Church has invoked her full teaching authority. But, even if there were a close call in one instance or another, one's judgment is in large part dependent on one's inclination. The inclination entailed in the vow of obedience is to put the best possible interpretation on the teaching in question, to give the benefit of the doubt, to accent as best one can, within the bounds of reason and honesty, the continuities rather than the discontinuities. One makes no apology for this inclination or disposition. One wants to defend as best one can the Magisterium and respect for its authority. Pope means "papa," and because one loves the family one defends the father of the family, especially when he is under attack from within and without. There is a virtue in defending one's own. It is called loyalty. Not blind loyalty, but loyalty with eyes wide open.

In 1990, the Congregation for the Doctrine of the Faith issued a document that has received much less attention than it deserves. *The Ecclesial Vocation of the Theologian* underscores, as the title suggests, that the Catholic theologian is not a free-lancer but a participant in the teaching ministry of the Church. Theologians do not constitute a parallel magisterium or, as some claim, a "loyal opposition" to the Magisterium, but a necessary partnership in preserving and transmitting the truth entrusted to the Church—a truth that the people who are the

Church have a right to receive in its uncompromised integrity. Among the remarkable things in *Ecclesial Vocation* is its candor in admitting that the Magisterium does not always teach as adequately or as clearly as it should. That is why theologians are necessary. They also have a critical role, keeping in mind that criticism is always in the service of helping the Magisterium to fulfill its responsibility more effectively.

There is even room for "dissent" when dissent means pointing out inadequacies that call for greater clarity or elaboration in an exercise of teaching. In magisterial documents of the pontificate of John Paul II, John Henry Newman is cited as a model of the ecclesial theologian. Before the definition of infallibility in 1870, Newman was an "inopportunist"; that is, he did not oppose the doctrine but believed that it was not opportune, that it might do considerable damage, to define it at that time at the highest level of the Church's teaching authority. When it was defined by Vatican Council I, however, he readily gave his assent. His previous judgment was overruled. Unlike some theologians today who are frequently self-described as dissenters, he did not organize resistance to the teaching, never mind go to the Catholic people or the general media to promote opposition to magisterial teaching.

The pontificate of John Paul II was frequently depicted as rigorous and oppressive, with Cardinal Ratzinger, now Benedict XVI, as "the doctrinal enforcer" clamping down on anyone who ventured an unconventional thought. In fact, during years of rampant dissent publicly flaunted, probably no more than twelve theologians were formally called on the carpet for their writings. Most clarified what they had written, and a couple were disciplined. Upon being disciplined, the American theologian

Matthew Fox, who was into the worship of the gods and goddesses of deep eco-theology, took out a full page advertisement in the *New York Times* in which he solicited financial contributions under the headline, "I HAVE BEEN SILENCED!" Some silencing. Fox later became an Episcopalian and then the guru of a center for Creation Spirituality in the Bay Area. Many Catholics thought the pontificate of John Paul was not only far from being rigorously oppressive but altogether too lax in ensuring that Catholic theologians do indeed teach what the Church teaches.

Without doubt the most lionized theological dissident since the Council was Father Hans Küng of Tübingen University in Germany. With the help of a team of collaborators he had for years published a stream of books, some of them bestsellers, assaulting what he depicted as the mendacity and corruption of the Magisterium and proposing radically revisionist views of Catholic faith and morals. After many efforts to engage him in constructive conversation, which he adamantly rejected, Rome finally withdrew his certification as a Catholic theologian, although he was not excommunicated and remained a priest. Küng and his many followers predictably portrayed him as the premier victim of Vatican authoritarianism.

In 1988, I invited Cardinal Ratzinger to deliver the annual Erasmus Lecture sponsored by *First Things*, which included a two-day ecumenical theological conference in New York. During the meeting, Ratzinger, who is in person gentle and self-effacing, reflected on the Church's discipline of theologians, citing Küng as a case in point. Küng had for years, he said, been declaring publicly that he did not teach what the Catholic Church teaches. He had rejected repeated pleas to discuss his differences with the appropriate office of the Magisterium, the Congregation for the Doctrine of the Faith. What CDF finally had to do, said Ratzinger, was to say in effect, "Dear Father Hans, we deeply regret that you have finally convinced us that you are right. You persist in saying that your positions are not those of the Catholic Church. We therefore, and very reluctantly, agree with you. You are not a Catholic theologian. It would be gravely misleading for the Church to continue to certify you as such."

The consequences for Küng were mild. He lost the university chair that was reserved for a church-certified theologian, but another position was promptly created for him and, with his team of collaborators, he did not miss a beat in continuing his assaults on the Magisterium. The CDF decision further enhanced, for a time, his celebrity as the world's foremost persecuted dissident. But at least now it was on the record that he did not speak for the Church as a Catholic theologian. And after a while, deprived of the drama of seeing how far one could go and still be a Catholic theologian, interest in what a German professor at Tübingen had to say dramatically waned. One notes with interest that in the first months of his pontificate, Benedict invited Father Küng to dinner and four hours of one-on-one conversation. It is said to have been a cordial meeting, and it demonstrates once again—as everyone who knows him already knew—that Benedict combines a gentle dialogical spirit with an uncompromising commitment to the truth entrusted to the Church.

In the United States there have been similar cases, although involving thinkers of less distinction. I have already mentioned Matthew Fox. In 1990, Father Charles Curran, a moral theologian who had played a major part in orchestrating the rejection of *Humanae Vitae*, lost his final appeal to be reinstated as a professor at Catholic University in Washington, D.C. He now teaches at Southern Methodist University. Others have escaped official censure largely because, or so it is said, it would only draw attention to them. They typically represent themselves as the tribunes of alienated Catholics, and their dissent is expressed as "loyal opposition" to an allegedly calcified and oppressive ecclesiastical leadership.

To call the pope a reactionary idiot, as some dissidents do, is very rude but it is not heresy. These people are faithfully on call for television talk shows about things Catholic. Tenured professors of a mischievous bent aim to shock by suggesting that, for instance, Mary was not a virgin—well, not literally a virgin—and Jesus married Mary Magdalene, fathered children, and is buried in Galilee. After a few decades the fun of shock theology is reduced somewhat because people who have never been catechized don't know what is supposed to be shocking. In any event, such antics are viewed more as naughty than as a serious challenge to magisterial teaching. Meanwhile, many Catholics are misled about the Church's teaching, and many others wonder why these theologians are not censured. The answer to the latter question is no doubt related to church authorities who think they have enough problems without precipitating a media furor by censoring maverick priests and academics. Prudence is the polite word commonly invoked in this connection.

The conservative Catholic press regularly complains that dissidents should have the honesty to leave the Church if they don't believe what she teaches. On this score, Martin Luther is often proposed as a model of integrity, and there is back-handed praise for such as Matthew Fox who shake the Catholic dust from their feet and establish their own religions. One answer to the conservative complaint, however, is that most of these people have nowhere else to go, or at least nowhere else where they would have an audience and organizing base. Rosemary Radford Reuther was a prominent radical in the 1960s who promoted a theology of eco-feminist-liberationism that bore scant resemblance to the Catholic faith. Asked why she did not leave the Church, she memorably responded, "Because that's where the mimeograph machines are."

The reference to mimeograph machines decidedly dates a show, *The Radical Post–Vatican II Church*, that has been running for a very long time. It closed on Broadway years ago, but a revival is always playing somewhere in the back streets of the big world that is Catholicism. In truth, at almost any given time in New York there are off-off-Broadway plays with generic titles such as *Sister Mary Ignatius Explains It All for You*. These inevitably feature grim authoritarian nuns cracking knuckles with their rulers and reminding us of the bad old "pre–Vatican II Church" from which we have been liberated. For the most part, they play to declining audiences of people who can remember the bad old days, or heard about them from their grandparents.

It is not true, as some Protestants console themselves by saying, that the Catholic theological circumstance is as anarchic as that of, say, the Episcopal or ELCA Lutheran churches, or as the multifarious theological worlds of evangelicalism. Despite all, the center holds, however precarious the hold might sometimes seem. Even the most clamorous dissidents know what they are dissenting from. They typically are not freelancers but embittered traditionalists who have a long tradition of trying to change the Church's tradition. They are, in their cantankerously discontented way, ecclesial theologians. They are outraged by, not indifferent to, admonitory instructions from the Congregation for the Doctrine of the Faith. They resent it when the magisterial parent tries to discipline her unruly children, but the acknowledgment that the Magisterium is the parent is essential to the rebellion. They fervently declare their anticipatory obedience to the next pope or the next council or to the pope and council after that, confident that the parent will at last come around to agreeing with them. They would be at a complete loss were the parent simply to abdicate authority. For the habitually dissident, too, ecclesial authority provides a secure identity.

It would be a mistake to exaggerate the role of dissidence in Catholic theology. True, the annual meeting of the Catholic Theological Society of America sometimes seems to be only vestigially Catholic. It would not be too far off the mark to say it is Catholic by virtue of the institutions that employ its members. But that is an academic guild, and it is the way of academic guilds to be neophiliac in their obsession with what is new and "creative." Revisionism, deconstructionism, iconoclasm—such are the routinized ways to gain peer notice and advancement. For all its talk about being a parallel magisterium or, in its more radical modes, revolutionizing Catholic faith and life, the academic guild knows that it is not in charge. It is also a mistake to underestimate the number of theologians who have wearied of dissident games, or were never attracted to them in the first place. They know that the great truths of the faith are much more exciting than the latest twists and turns of critical theory, and they devote their lives to the high spiritual and intellectual adventure of transmitting to the next generation "the faith once delivered to the saints."

Conservatives will continue to complain about dissident theologians who are vainly striving to achieve the gravitas of heresy. As well they should. That, in no little part, is what conservatives are for. And parents will continue to complain about sending their children to Catholic colleges and universities only to have their faith deconstructed. As well they should. And bishops will continue to pay lip service to *Ex Corde Ecclesiae*, the 1990 constitution advancing the controversial proposition that Catholic higher education should be Catholic. *Ex Corde Ecclesiae* means "from the heart of the Church," and from the trembling hearts of bishops will continue to come reason after reason for avoiding confrontation with academic institutions or anyone else. After all, they say, theirs is a ministry of unity. And they are right about that, in part.

The Magisterium of the Church presides rather than controls. The pope claims universal and immediate jurisdiction over the Church, but nobody should think that he and his few hundred aides in the Roman Curia can control the hundreds of thousands of bishops, priests, theologians, and teachers of all sorts who are charged with the responsibility of guarding and transmitting the faith. The Magisterium demarcates and to some extent patrols the outer boundaries of the permissible, and occasionally disciplines egregious offenders. It provides authoritative and readily accessible points of reference such as the 1994 *Catechism of the Catholic Church*. The Magisterium raises the flag at the center that holds, to which the confused and pedagogically abused can repair.

But the Magisterium, including the entire college of bishops, can do only so much. Finally, the guarding and transmitting of the faith depends upon the assent and fidelity of those who are charged with the task, and assent and fidelity, if they are authentic, must be free. Bishops are right, in part, when they say theirs is a ministry of unity and not of confrontation. Unity that is unity in the truth, however, requires that teachers of the faith be confronted with the opportunity to freely pledge their assent and fidelity. Those who cannot or will not do so can be helped to understand the falsity of their position, and why elementary self-respect should lead them to find another line of work. If they claim that they must stay because they are the Magisterium and must rescue the Church from the pseudo-Magisterium of the pope and bishops, they must, gently if possible, be deprived of their delusions of self-importance.

Even were the theologians and teachers of the Church more faithful or more constructively discipled, or simply more competent, the Catholic theological situation would be wondrously diverse. The deposit of faith as defined by the Magisterium is one thing; theological reflections on that one thing are various, much as jazz or a Bach fugue or paintings of the Madonna are variations on a theme. The Church is not a school of any one theology; she is the mother of theologies. This is frequently a scandal to those on their way to becoming Catholic. Lutheranism is an ecclesial structure built on a school of theology, namely, that of Martin Luther and his followers. The church called Calvinism was constructed on the foundation of John Calvin's theology. And so forth.

Different theologies required different churches. That was, and to a large extent still is, the Protestant way. In my experience,

Protestants on the way to becoming Catholic frequently want to be assured that their school of theology is agreed to, or at least permitted, by the Catholic Church. That is, I believe, an understandable but finally misguided concern. The Catholic Church is not in question. The Catholic Church does not have to pass the test of ways of thinking that occasioned schism from the Catholic Church. If one is a Lutheran, a Calvinist, a Wesleyan, or whatever, one does not become a Catholic only to continue to be the Protestant that one was. Of course, people bring with them whatever is worthy in the traditions by which they were formed. Again, all the grace and truth to be found outside the boundaries of the Catholic Church gravitate toward unity with the Catholic Church.

In becoming Catholic, however, one enters a wondrously and sometimes confusingly capacious universe of faith, prayer, piety, and forms of discipleship. As G. K. Chesterton observed, the Catholic Church is so much larger from the inside than from the outside. One enters in order to be changed. One is changed by Mary and Marian devotion, for a very big and transforming instance. One is changed by leaving behind the tortured introspection about one's spiritual state and entering into the crisp objectivity of sins unambiguously confessed and unambiguously forgiven in the Sacrament of Reconciliation. One is changed by the example and company of monastics who demonstrate the diverse ways of radical discipleship and how it is that some Christians are more advanced in holiness, and some become the saints we are all called to be. One is changed by popular devotions to Our Lady and the saints that in their unbounded exuberance touch upon more things in heaven and earth than are dreamt of in the stammerings of our theological systems. One is changed by mystics and miracles and could-be superstitions given the benefit of the doubt. One is changed by priestly power to transform bread into body and wine into blood, by God's submitting Himself to be delivered and adored. One is changed by the theological suspension of one's theories of the Church and surrendering oneself to the Church that does not need one's theories in order to be. One enters in order to be changed.

To say that the center holds is to say, in part, that the Magisterium is an anchor. But it is also a compass. Both anchor and compass are needed, depending upon the turbulence of the surrounding sea. The Church is called the barque of Peter on its way to the destination of the promised Kingdom. In the third eucharistic prayer we ask God "to strengthen in faith and love your pilgrim Church on earth." The images speak of stability and movement, of communal identity through time. Employing the nautical imagery, the Magisterium is in command on the bridge. One may be asked to help out from time to time, but one is not in charge. In a different turn on that image, Newman said that, all in all, he was very happy in the barque of Peter, and he was happier the farther he was from the engine room. Those on the bridge and in the engine room have their appointed tasks and, we are assured, the charisms necessary for carrying them out. As do we all. We are pilgrims and passengers and members of the crew beckoned onward by what the Church calls "the universal call to holiness." Which is to say, beckoned on by Christ and the promise of the Kingdom. What is expected of us is to respond to the call where we are, and in doing so to allow ourselves to be carried where we are to be.

People on the way to becoming Catholic frequently raise objections about the current state of Catholicism. They don't know the half of it. It is one thing to desire to be part of the Church of Jesus Christ most fully and rightly ordered through time, but quite another to brace oneself for the vacuity and disorder so widespread in the Church today. It helps a little to be reminded that it was probably always so. But only a little. In the thirteenth century, "age of faith" peasants contrived to purloin the consecrated host to apply as a poultice on the sores of sick cattle. A gross superstition, no doubt, but at least it is interesting. It is not that the interestingly bizarre is entirely absent today. In my parish there is an elderly woman who really does believe in the Holy Quaternity, although she doesn't put it that way. She was much taken with, and mistaken about, a homily in which I explained why we call Mary the Mother of God. I obviously did not explain it very well, for this dear woman thanked me for confirming what she has always believed: There is no point in praying to the son when you can go directly to the mother. I no longer try very hard to correct her. God will no doubt sort out her prayers.

The bizarre is not to be found only among the uneducated. A philosophy professor who thinks of himself as conservative subscribes to a radical notion of papal infallibility. He tells me that, if the pope declared that $2+2=5$, he would immediately give the proposition his unqualified assent. Instances such as these do not rise to the dignity of heresy, but they do remind us that the piety and imagination of the millions of people who are the Church constitute a potpourri of wondrous confusions insouciantly indifferent to the magisterial definition of "the structure of faith." To be a Catholic is to refuse to hold oneself aloof from the vulgar, which is usually simply another word for the popular.

The great problem is not the popular piety of traditional devotions but the things that have been imposed by experts over recent decades. This is notably true with respect to liturgy and music. For most of these changes there was slight popular demand and considerable popular resistance; but they are now part of Catholic life in most parishes, and there is limited evidence of relief in sight. When one puts oneself up for adoption by the Church, when one is admitted to the family, among the first shocks is discovering how busily people have been getting rid of the family treasures. And the new acquisitions, such as liturgy in the vernacular, are frequently so shoddy. Father George Rutler, a noted pastor in Manhattan and a former Episcopalian, is regularly asked whether he misses anything since he became a Catholic. He just as regularly answers: "Oh yes. I do so miss the liturgy in English." When the Second Vatican Council permitted the liturgy in the vernacular—contra many liturgists, it did not mandate the vernacular—slap-dash translations of the Latin were rushed into use. Numerous scholars, and authorities in Rome, have complained about the inaccuracy of the translations; but, if it is possible, their inaccuracy is outdone by their spectacular banality. Many of the appointed prayers may fairly be summarized in the petition, "O Lord, help us to be even nicer people than we already are." Awe, majesty, mystery, unworthiness—anything associated with wonder in the face of the numinous—is out. Familiarity, good feelings, and self-congratulation are in.

The bare ruined choirs are not beyond repair. Many, as did Pope Benedict when he was Cardinal Ratzinger, speak of the pressing need for a "reform of the reform." To understand what that might mean, however, it is helpful to understand what went wrong, and what went right, with the reforms in the aftermath of the Council.

5 | Lest Catholics Be Different

Anyone thinking about becoming Catholic is forewarned. Must reading is a little book by Thomas Day, a modern classic, *Why Catholics Can't Sing: The Culture of Catholicism and the Triumph of Bad Taste*. It is both comic and sad. Cradle Catholics read it laughing through their tears. Converts brace themselves. Day sends up chatty priests who emcee the Mass as though it were their own live talk show, song leaders who challenge anyone else to sing, and happy-clappy ditties that might embarrass preschoolers. There is, to cite but one of hundreds, "To Be Alive":

> *To be alive and feeling free*
> *And to have everyone in your family*
> *To be alive in every way*
> *Oh how great it is*
> *To be alive.*

Be forewarned. "Convert stories" have been a major genre in Catholic popular literature. That has been less so in recent years because, as we have seen, some Catholics assume there is a tension, even a contradiction, between ecumenism and conversion. "Why," it is asked, "would you want to become a Catholic when we Catholics have only now learned how wonderful Lutheranism is?" There are compelling theological reasons for becoming Catholic. Not so long ago, convert stories typically stressed the compelling aesthetic attractions of Catholicism. People such as Thomas Merton were drawn to the Church by the beauty, the solemnity, the ceremony, the dignity of the worship. The word commonly used was "mystery."

Merton, writing a long while ago, described the genius of Gregorian chant:

> *It is an austere warmth, the warmth of Gregorian chant. It is deep beyond ordinary emotion, and that is one reason why you never get tired of it. It never wears you out by making a lot of cheap demands on your sensibilities. Instead of drawing you out into the open field of feelings where your enemies, the devil and your own imagination and the inherent vulgarity of your own corrupted nature, can get at you with their blades and cut you to pieces, it draws you within, where you are lulled in peace and recollection and where you find God.[1]*

"Cheap demands on your sensibilities" nicely describes the experience of much contemporary liturgy and music. One now more commonly encounters people who, instead of being attracted by the beauty of it all, entered the Church despite the aesthetic shambles of liturgy and music in many parishes. For the "high church" Lutheran or Episcopalian, contemporary Catholicism can be a liturgical and musical move downmarket, and sometimes way down. When over lunch I told my editor friend Norman Podhoretz, with whom I share musical passions, that I was becoming a Catholic, there was at first a long pause. Then, with a deeply baffled expression, "But, Richard, what about Bach?" What about Bach indeed.

As I say, anyone thinking about becoming Catholic should brace himself by reading Thomas Day's *Why Catholics Can't Sing*. That having been said, I do believe the silliest of the silly season is past or now passing. And I am impressed by Lutherans and Anglicans who, upon entering into full communion, say they are pleasantly surprised to find that the horror stories of Catholic worship are greatly exaggerated. You can still find, here and there, priests who pin balloons to their vestments, ad lib the words of the Mass as though it were their personal performance, and never rise homiletically above "Have a nice day." There are still the ditties of doggerel set to vapid tunes that would make even Andrew Lloyd Webber wince; ditties that are typically much more about Wonderful, Wonderful Us than about the glory of the Lord. But all that is now passing. Its passing is hastened by the complaints of lay people who go to Mass not to celebrate their wonderful selves but to surrender themselves in the worship of the Mystery who is Christ in his Real Presence. Avery Cardinal Dulles tells of saying Mass in a parish that had a big banner by the altar emblazoned with the message, "God is Other People." He says he very much wished that he had had a magic marker with which to put a big comma after "Other." But that, he notes, was more than twenty years ago.

Stories of liturgical and musical malpractice abound. Where Catholics gather to lament the state of the Church, the game of choice is "Can you top this?" It can be very funny, in a sad sort of way. The malpractice is evident not only in liturgical and musical antics but also in the bare ruined choirs of churches stripped to the austere specifications of "worship spaces" designed to facilitate the community's encounter with itself. Encounter with the Other is a decidedly secondary consideration, if it is considered at all. The tabernacle of the Real Presence is moved either somewhere off to the side or into a closet-sized space down a side corridor, as though to pose a challenge to those really determined to engage in eucharistic adoration. Not for nothing are the church renovations of recent decades sometimes referred to as wreckovations. All this is painfully true, and there will no doubt be cause for legitimate complaint far into the future. However . . .

There is a real and present danger of idealizing the state of liturgy and music prior to the destabilizations following the Council. Today's reformers rightly remind us that the preconciliar twenty-minute "quickie Mass" hurriedly mumbled in butchered Latin to get people in and out with minimum delay was not marked by the aesthetic care or reverence that so many say they miss today. The Council called for full, active, and conscious participation by the faithful. "Active" was sometimes interpreted as a mandate for keeping the people busy.

A liturgist recently reported that he observed a Mass with stopwatch in hand and discovered that 80 percent of the time the people were not *doing* anything. I expect some of them were just praying, or pondering the mystery of what God was doing at and on the altar. After the Council, liturgical experts obsessed with change imposed novelty upon novelty, the result being the radical destabilization of the sacramental and devotional order. But again, that season is passing. Today, the new thing is the recovery of the traditional. It is commonly called "the reform of the reform," and it is making headway, albeit too slowly. Balloons, priests in clown outfits, and the guitar-strumming monotony of "Kumbaya my Lord" are period pieces; they are embarrassingly remembered by aging baby boomers, and utterly baffling to their children and grandchildren.

Then, too, and despite the banality and sentimentality of the English texts that were rushed into use for the New Order Mass *(Novus Ordo Missae)*, it is a rite that can be done, and often is done, with dignity, reverence, and more than a touch of the majesty that befits the worship of God. And, let it be admitted, the banality and the sentimentality chiefly offend those of us who were reared in the elegantly virile liturgical English of *The Book of Common Prayer.* That was also the language adopted by Lutherans in this country when they switched from their immigrant tongues. After the Council, the general Catholic experience was very different. They went from the linguistic obscurity of the Latin to the linguistic barbarism of the New Order without passing through civilized English. Most Catholics, the former Episcopalian Father Rutler tells me, simply don't know what he is talking about when he says he misses the liturgy in English.

And yet there is this: the attentive reverence of Catholics at the eucharistic prayer, and most notably at the consecration and elevation of the elements. At least that is, with notable exceptions, my experience. It is so intense that you can, so to speak, cut it with a knife. Despite all the chatter about the Mass as a celebration of the wonderful people that we are, there is this almost electric intensity of devotion toward what God is doing, toward the reality that Christ is keeping his promise once again when we "do this" in remembrance of him. Or so I have found it to be in parishes around the country, in corrugated huts in the slums of Mexico City, in the basilicas of Rome, in a bombed-out schoolhouse in Nigeria, in a Polish priory, in a village church of northern Quebec. Such palpable intensity of devotion, such manifest evidence of being caught up into the Mystery, I did not see in all my years as a Lutheran. It is quiet, undemonstratively earnest, a palpable yearning for a gift desired, a sigh of gratitude for a gift received. "It" is happening again. It is the Mass that holds together the maddeningly ragtag and variegated thing that is the Catholic Church. Which is to say it is the Presence. Which is to say it is Christ, doing it again, just as he promised.

For this one will readily sacrifice a great deal. The aesthetic sacrifice is not a matter of *mere* aesthetics. As the great Hans Urs von Balthasar underscored, the aesthetic is inseparable from the encounter with the beauty of being, and of Being. Balthasar is much read and much discussed in seminaries today, but it will not be easy to remedy the liturgical and musical consequences of the reckless experimentation following the Council. If there is to be a remedy, it will be the work of a generation or two, or more. In the early twentieth century leading up to the Council, there was a powerful movement for liturgical renewal. As a Lutheran seminarian in the 1950s, I read avidly *The Liturgical Renaissance in the Roman Catholic Church* by Ernest Koenker, a Lutheran. The Christian world, but especially Lutherans and Anglicans, looked with high hope to what was happening in Catholicism. The renaissance in question was not about liturgical niceties in any narrow or fussy sense, but about the recovery of mystery and wonder, reappropriating the world of the arts, and communicating the excitement of the Christian way of being in the world through effective preaching and catechesis.

There were those whom we viewed as giants: Romano Guardini, Odo Casel, Josef Jungmann, Friedrich Heiler, Virgil Michel. There was the former Protestant, Louis Bouyer, who wrote marvelous books on liturgical form, monasticism, and the spirituality of the sacramental life. In St. Louis there was Monsignor Martin Hellriegel of Holy Cross Church. A kindly pioneer of the renaissance in America, Hellriegel was always hospitable to the students of Concordia Seminary, and he opened to me and many other Lutheran seminarians the vision of a parish come fully alive. In my many years at St. John the Evangelist in the inner city of Brooklyn, the pastoral inspiration of Msgr. Hellriegel was never far from my mind. He and others, such as Father Louis Bouyer, lived to be very old and witnessed the postconciliar wreckage of the renaissance they had pioneered. They shook their heads sadly, saying, "That is not what we meant. That is not what we meant at all."

Across the room where I write I spot the five-volume work of Pius Parsch, *The Church's Year of Grace*. It is a winsome and deep exploration of the sanctifying of time through the Church's calendar. It is now a period piece, a curiosity, a guide to what used to be. In recent decades, holy days of obligation have been largely eliminated, great feasts such as Epiphany and Ascension have been transferred to the nearest convenient Sunday, the twelve days of Christmas are no more, the season of Epiphany has been eliminated, as has the pre-Lenten season, replaced by "Sundays in Ordinary Time." The phrase "ordinary time" has a technical meaning for liturgists, but in the vernacular it suggests something else. The entire argument of *The Church's Year of Grace* is that no time is ordinary. The pioneers of the renaissance were pushed aside as new reformers in a hurry set about their task of banalizing, flattening, and making ordinary what had been Catholicism's worlds within worlds of sacramental and artistic wonder. (Although Ascension and Epiphany have been moved to the nearest convenient Sunday, one may be grateful that Ash Wednesday and Good Friday are still, respectively, on Wednesday and Friday.)

It was as though the reformers were embarrassed by what was distinctively Catholic. There was a seemingly little thing that, probably as much as any one change, undermined Catholic identity: rescinding the rule of the Friday abstinence. It was not an onerous rule. As Jews did not eat pork, so Catholics did not eat meat on Friday. Catholics understood it and everybody else understood it. It was one of those things that came with being Catholic. It was easily explained: Self-denial, even if modest, is an important part of the Christian life; and Friday is the day on which Our Lord gave up all and we give up a little in gratitude for his giving up all. There was no popular demand that the rule be rescinded. But in 1966 it was, leading many Catholics to wonder what other elements that once seemed constitutive of being Catholic might be up for grabs.

Abstinence on Fridays during Lent is still the rule, but for the rest of the year it is optional. And even fasting is not what was once understood by fasting. Now it means small meals and no snacks, and people younger than eighteen and older than sixty are exempted. And abstinence from meat is prescribed for Ash

Wednesday and Good Friday, only two days out of the year. An act of penance on Fridays is limply recommended, and spottily observed by the few Catholics who are aware of the recommendation. Almost anything—taking out the garbage, for instance—qualifies as an act of penance. It was officially explained at the time that it is much better for people to do something voluntarily and not because it is a rule. That is a very Protestant way of thinking that elevates the voluntary above practices of communal solidarity. Abstinence and fasting became a matter of choice in a pervasively prochoice society. The voluntary, the optional, the hesitantly recommended quickly fall into desuetude.

Eamon Duffy, the distinguished Cambridge historian of Christianity, writes that this is no little matter.[2] From at least the end of the first century, Christians observed Fridays, and later the forty days of Lent, as fast days remembering the Passion of the Christ. "At the heart of Catholicism for a millennium and a half lay the dialectic dividing of time, a rhythmic movement between the poles of fast and feast, Lent and Easter, renunciation and affirmation." Catholicism, Duffy says, is committing "ritual suicide," with large consequences for communal identity and spiritual discipline. There was also a powerful link between fasting and a Catholic sense of being dislocated in ordinary space and time. Fasting reminds Christians that they are people of the cross, and is, however inadequately, an acted-out statement of solidarity with the poor and hungry of the world.

Especially limp was the explanation of the English bishops upon the abandonment of the tradition. They noted that in today's world many people have their main meal at work and that there are often Friday social events at which abstinence puts Catholics in an awkward position. Wrote the bishops: "While an alternative dish is often available, it is questioned whether it is advisable in our mixed society for a Catholic to appear singular in this matter. Non-Catholics know and accept that we do not eat meat on Fridays, but often they do not understand why we do not, and in consequence regard us as odd." Oh dear, people may think us odd and singular. If people do not understand what we do and do not do, one might have expected the bishops to note that this presents a wonderful opportunity to explain and, in doing so, bear winsome witness to our faith. But no, the important thing is that Catholics not be put in an awkward position, that they fit in, that, if others discover that we are, incidentally, Catholics, they can be reassured that we are just like everybody else.

When the American bishops announced the change of the Friday abstinence rule, they avoided the defensiveness of their English confreres. The American statement indicated that the bishops assumed most Catholics would continue to abstain on Fridays. They even felt it necessary to caution Catholics not to look down on those who now chose some different penitential discipline. The bishops obviously overestimated the solidity of the tradition, with respect to abstinence and much else. Within weeks, most Catholics were enjoying hotdogs and steaks on Friday, and the practice of alternative forms of Friday discipline were not conspicuous. The message received by the majority of Catholics was that the Friday rule had been repealed. The truth is that abstention from meat on Fridays had been made optional. It was now a matter of choice. When it comes to traditions that sustain a sense of communal identity, making something optional is tantamount to repealing it. Again, being a Catholic meant, among many other things, that you did not eat meat on Friday the way being a Jew means, among many other things, that you don't eat pork. It came with being Catholic. Being a Catholic and doing the things that Catholics do was not a matter of individual election but of being among the elect.

What was behind the dismantling and destabilizing of so much that had constituted a Catholic culture? To hear some traditionalists tell it, the enemies of the Church exploited the Council to seize control of the leverages of power and decision-making. Even Pope Paul VI, in one of his many melancholy moods, spoke about detecting "the smoke of Satan" in the post-conciliar Church. In this country, several dynamics were hard at work. An immigrant Catholicism was poignantly eager to demonstrate that it had really arrived in America. Remember that the Council came in the immediate aftermath of the election of John F. Kennedy, *the* symbolic marker, after a long history of anti-Catholicism in America, that Catholics are as American as anybody else.

A 1985 textbook still widely used, *The American Catholic Experience*, is the tale of a success story ending on the triumphant note that Catholics are now more or less like everybody else. They had at last escaped the much reviled Catholic "ghetto." The shedding of Catholic distinctives, the liberation from what made Catholics different, the assimilation to a majority Protestant society—such dynamics help explain the dismantling and destabilizing of Catholic culture. Then too, there was the Council's affirmation of ecumenism. I have no doubt that the ecumenical move was at the direction of the Holy Spirit. There is also no doubt that the misunderstanding of ecumenism led many Catholics to believe that differences were to be down-played, that what were once deep differences now made no difference, that Catholicism was one denominational option among others.

I enjoy talking with older Catholics, priests and lay people, and listen to their tales of how things used to be. Yes, this is largely an exercise in nostalgia, but there is nothing wrong with nostalgia, moderately indulged. And it is worth remembering that, in not many years, we, too, will be the stuff of other peoples' nostalgia. Listening to our elders is also an exercise in respect for lives lived faithfully and, by many, heroically. We listen not to turn back the clock, although it is obviously wrong to say, as we often hear, that you cannot turn back the clock. We do it all the time when clocks are telling the wrong time. Talking with older Catholics helps us to reestablish the baseline by which we can measure the changes that have happened, for better and for worse. Perhaps most of us can remember pestering our parents to tell us about "the olden days," about the world as it was when they were young, about the world as it was before we were born. For some of us that means the 1930s or the 1950s, and for those of us of a certain age it comes as something of a shock to realize that, for most young people today, it means the 1980s and 1990s.

Archie Dinoia, eighty-two years old and long retired, was an executive with IT&T, a major communications company. He has given me permission to write about the way he remembers being Catholic some sixty or seventy years ago.[3] Of course, a Catholic boyhood in Union City, New Jersey, is not *the* baseline by which to measure subsequent changes. Catholic boyhoods were lived over the centuries in places as various as Antioch,

Buenos Aires, Bagdhad, Milan, Warsaw, Manila, County Cork, and the farms of Wisconsin. But Archie Dinoia remembers *a* baseline, a time and place of Catholic faith and clarity that will, I expect, be recognized by most cradle Catholics of a certain age. It is important that we remember those times and places, for they are the stories of Catholicism in America as it was not so very long ago. Without these stories, we will not understand Catholicism as it is, and as it may become.

The main thing, says Archie, the really big thing, is that, as a Catholic, you knew that you had been entrusted with the truth and it was the entire purpose of your life to live according to it:

We were the heirs of 1,900 years of martyrdoms, fastings, prayers, vigils, hair shirts, masses, pilgrimages, speculations, contemplations, and the making of saints. The sufferings and trials and tribulations were behind us. Ours was the treasury of the piled up graces of all the good works of the Catholic people over the centuries. We had all the answers, we really did, and far from being embarrassed in saying that, it was our proudest boast. How could we seriously question the wisdom accumulated under the guidance of the Holy Spirit over 1,900 years? Why should we want to? Our business was to learn it, give our assent, and try to live accordingly.

Most vividly he remembers the daily early Mass:

It was before most people had automobiles and as a young boy I marveled at all the old ladies—they were probably in their fifties or sixties—wrapped in their black shawls and plodding down the streets that were deserted, except for a few men

*delivering the milk, in a hurry not to be late for the early
Mass. In the winter, the streets were still dark and the church
was dark and hushed, with only the flickering candles around
the altar and the statues of the saints. The statues of the saints
and angels welcomed us to come and pray with them, glad to
see us after their lonely all-night vigil.*

Archie remembers the early Mass at the "Blue Chapel"
maintained for a community of cloistered Dominican nuns. It
was plastered all in blue and had a white marble altar and rere-
dos that seemed to reach to the heavens. The nuns were hidden
behind a dark screen to the side of the altar. "I knew they were
there because I could hear the rustling of the rosary beads and
the occasional cough, and I knew how many they were by
counting the hosts distributed through the small opening in the
screen. There were so many of them, and they were all praying
for us and for all the unhappy people in an unhappy world."
The sorrow of things, the *lacrimae rerum*, was pervasively present. Young Archie understood that we are all passing through
this veil of tears. The laughter and the joy of being Catholic was
in knowing that God had provided the Church and sacraments
to see us through to an infinitely better place.

*Promptly at six-thirty the bell would ring and the priest
would enter, approach the altar, and begin his murmurings
with his back to us and his face to God. We all faced God in
those days. I don't object to the vernacular, to the Mass in
English. Now we can understand what is being said, but
there are so many words, and we are expected to pay
attention to each one. Words, words, words. Do we need so*

many words to speak with God? Now we are always being talked to, talked at.

Archie understood that the Church, the bishops, and the priests, needed a lot of words to guard the truth given by God.

But for us it was enough to know the Church was guarding the Truth, and the most important truth was always Truth in the upper case. What the Church taught we believed. Of course we didn't question. Why should we? How could the Church established by Jesus Christ teach error? If the Catholic Church did not teach the Truth, it is not the one true Church; and if it is not the one true Church, then Jesus Christ is not God; and if Jesus Christ is not God, there is no God. My friends and I all understood that. The truth didn't depend upon our understanding all the words the Church used to guard the truth. Credo in unam, sanctam, catholicam et apostolicam Ecclesiam. We believe in one, holy, catholic, and apostolic Church.

A theologian might wince at the possible implication that the Church rather than Christ is the foundation of faith, but Archie Dinoia doesn't claim to be a theologian. As it happens, his way of putting the matter is, however intuitively, close to St. Augustine's statement, "I would not have believed the gospel had not the authority of the Church moved me." Whether in matters of religion, science, politics, or the living of everyday life, we all believe on the basis of authority more than most of us like to think. The systematically consistent skeptic who accepts nothing as true that he has not personally proved beyond a rational doubt would, if there is such a person, be incapable of getting out of bed in the morning. In theory, his skepticism may be relentlessly consistent (except for not being skeptical about his skepticism), but not in life.

Archie remembers that the daily Mass was hardly the end of it. The church remained open and at any time of day there were people kneeling at the altar rail or at the feet of the statue of Mary or of their favorite saint.

There was the depression and then the terrible war. Maybe people had bigger needs then. If a husband lost a job or the house was about to be foreclosed or a son was in trouble with the law, all you had to do was make a visit to the church and ask for God's help. Of course He would help! The most important thing was the visit to Jesus in the tabernacle. I can't tell you how important that was. The tabernacle was always up high on the altar. The altar and the tabernacle, that was the center of everything. At Mass, Jesus was making himself present again, but he never left. He was always there in the tabernacle. The church building was like a tabernacle to contain the tabernacle. It was what the Bible calls the Holy of Holies, like in the temple in Jerusalem. The tabernacle, that's where Jesus Christ lives. At least that's what the nuns taught us, and boy did we ever believe it.

Actually receiving Christ at Communion was joy beyond measure, but also a matter of fear and trembling. "Of course we went to confession first." Every Saturday afternoon, from three until six, and in the evening from seven to nine, there were long lines and two or three or more priests hearing confession.

When Archie was nineteen and he and his buddies went into Manhattan for a night on the town, it seemed the natural thing that when they passed a church somebody would say, "Let's go to confession," and they all went in and got on line. This was not anticipatory absolution for whatever wrong they might do that night. It was a matter of taking every opportunity to keep the slate clean. "What if you committed a mortal sin and died that night? You could burn in hell forever."

"All that changed after the Council," says Archie.

The priests and bishops told us that the council fathers had decided we were going to confession too often. It seems we were all guilty of the sin of scrupulosity and didn't know it. They said we should only go to confession for very serious sins. I timidly asked the pastor, "You mean like mortal sin?" "No, no," he said, "you're still thinking in the old preconciliar categories." Very serious sin, I and millions of others concluded, had to do with bad dispositions and attitudes. Aside from obvious things like murder or adultery, it was pretty much up to us to decide whether we were guilty of serious sin. Some priests said that support for the Vietnam War or not caring enough about the environment counted as very, very serious sins. But for most of us the upshot of these changes was that we began to take a much more positive view of our spiritual state. If we weren't sinless, we were pretty close to it. Certainly we were most of the time, and for some of us all the time, innocent of serious sins. It got so that in church you almost never heard about sin any more. I guess it's no surprise that a lot of people thought that was a great improvement.

As the lines at the confessionals shortened or disappeared, the lines at communion became longer and longer. In some parishes, regular hours for confession were no longer posted. If you really had a crisis and needed to go, confession was "by appointment" at the parish office. Before the Council, about half the congregation would go up for communion at a Sunday Mass. We never gave a thought about why people refrained from communing. Maybe they hadn't gone to confession recently, or maybe they had broken the midnight fast. Remember that in those days the fast was from the previous midnight, not just one hour before Mass the way it is now. Or maybe they stayed back from communion because they felt they were not in a state of grace. "State of grace." It sounds almost quaint now, but then it was an absolute requirement for receiving the Body of Christ.

Now almost everybody receives; sometimes it seems like everybody. If you don't get in the communion line, you worry about getting funny looks. "He must really be guilty of something terrible." Who knows? But the point is that, if you don't commune, there must be something really wrong, like maybe you're guilty of serious sin.

Today it is generally agreed that there is no going back to the midnight fast, at least not as a rule applied to all, but the suggestion is heard that the one-hour fast be extended to three hours or at least two. That would make it somewhat more plausible to assume that those who do not commune had simply broken the fast. What Archie Dinoia remembers is a time when Catholics took more seriously the warning of St. Paul in I Corinthians 11: "Whoever, therefore, eats the bread or drinks the cup of the Lord in an unworthy manner will be guilty of profaning the body and blood of the Lord. Let a man examine himself, and so eat of the bread and drink of the cup. For any one who eats and drinks without discerning the body eats and drinks judgment upon himself."

That warning is featured prominently in John Paul II's encyclical of 2005, *Ecclesia de Eucharistia* (The Church of the Eucharist). But the warning goes up against almost half a century of a different piety and practice in which the accent is on the Eucharist as the community's festive meal to which all are welcome. It is frequently said today that the "body" to which St. Paul refers is the community, which is the body of Christ. Thus one bishop writes that when the priest or lay minister distributes the host with the words "The body of Christ," he should exchange a "deeply meaningful look" with the communicant so that it is understood that the words mean "*You* are the body of Christ." This is a fundamental shift in Catholic piety and sacramental practice. Of course the Church is the body of Christ, but she is that by virtue of the gift of Christ, as in the body of Christ in the Eucharist. *I* am not the body of Christ. I participate in the body of Christ by virtue of the gift that is given. In the Eucharist we are gathered not to celebrate our amazing selves and what we are doing but to be incorporated into the mystery of what Christ is doing. What Christ is doing and what we are doing are not to be separated; they are, however, to be clearly distinguished. It is a question of emphasis, but not *merely* of emphasis. The emphasis is all.[4]

There is more that Archie remembers. For instance, priests who were not reticent in addressing sexual morality from the pulpit:

All these years later, I recall a priest sternly reproaching men who were in the congregation for having violated someone's sister. He said we must respect the sisters of others, just as we expect them to respect our sisters. I suppose that sounds sexist today, but preaching like that was an important part of our moral education, and for the most part it took. I can't imagine hearing such a homily today. Somebody would be offended, and it seems the first and maybe only commandment today is "Thou shalt not give offense." Don't get me started on homilies. Most of them can be summed up in the assurance that we're all wonderful and we'd be even more wonderful if we recognized that everybody else is wonderful too. I don't want to exaggerate, but sometimes I have to wonder why Christ had to become man and suffer and die and go through all that agony because of our sins. So what's the big deal about sin? You wouldn't have a clue from the homilies preached today. All right, now I am exaggerating. But not by much.

Then there was High Mass, with the singers in the choir loft at the back of the church.

The first High Mass I remember was when I was about five years old, and I asked my mother who was singing. She told me it was the angels, and for years I pestered her to take me to High Mass so I could hear the angels. I didn't have the sense to turn around and look up at the choir loft. I was told the singers were at the back of the church so that they would not be a distraction, so that we keep our attention on what is happening at the altar. Many years later, the church was renovated and the statues of the saints were removed and taken God only knows where. The same reason was given: They were a distraction. But by then it was not clear what they would be a distraction from. I mean, now you had the song leader right up front, daring the congregation to match her high-decibel performance. And right up front were guitars, trumpets, and a piano, and a few times even dancers in tights. They're all competing for attention with a dozen lay ministers flitting around the altar. We're not supposed to notice everything going on?

I read where the lay people are called "extraordinary ministers of the Eucharist." There's nothing extraordinary about it at all. It is routine. Even at weekday Masses with only a few people you need all this help to give out communion? Maybe our priests are so delicate they can't distribute many communions, or maybe the people are in such a hurry to get out they can't abide the few extra minutes it would take for the priest to do what priests are supposed to do. I'm sorry. That may be unfair, but I can tell you there are a lot more distractions today with everybody getting in on the act and priests acting like ringmasters of the show. It was simpler and more focused when we just went to Mass and knew what was going to happen.

I expect Archie speaks for millions who remember how things used to be, as there are no doubt other millions of the same era who welcome the changes and think going to Mass is ever so much more interesting than it used to be. He is unhappy with the abolition of a dress code and remembers when people dressed for Mass in "their Sunday best." Others welcome the greater informality, but instinctively raise an eyebrow at the tee-shirts, tank tops, and women in very short shorts. Prior to the Council, there were also the popular devotions that played such a big part in personal and parish life, such as the Sacred Heart, Stations of the Cross, Rosary, and Benediction of the Blessed Sacrament.

Novenas—devotions with a special intention on nine successive days or the same day of nine successive weeks—were huge. "You should have seen the Monday Novena at St. Michael's Monastery in Union City," says Archie.

St. Michael's was the seminary of the Passionist order, and people came from all over. The place held a thousand people and was packed to the rafters. Week after week, the priest would announce the many prayers that had been answered, and at the side altars there were piles of canes and crutches and wheelchairs put there by people who had been healed. It was miracle time, and we believed it, and we loved it. Sure, we still have places like Lourdes and Fatima, but don't miracles happen in the parish anymore?

The textbooks by the liturgists tell us that such popular devotions were a substitute for meaningful participation in the liturgy of the Eucharist. Archie is among those who note that, after all the reforms, popular devotions have largely disappeared and participation in Mass has declined by more than half. *Post hoc ergo propter hoc?*

Signs of institutional decline are beyond dispute.

St. Michael's was a complex of fifty acres smack in the middle of Union City, which is at the New Jersey end of the Lincoln

Tunnel. The cupola was like St. Peter's in Rome. You could see it from Manhattan and the Jersey Turnpike and all over. There was a monumental Stations of the Cross on the property, and a graveyard for the Passionists who had died over the years. As a boy, I admired the priests and seminarians as they strolled the grounds reading their office with their Rosaries dangling on their cassocks. We were proud that that's where the Passionists put out the national magazine The Sign, which was very big. It went belly-up a long time ago. You can still see St. Michael's cupola from Manhattan. Now it's the Korean Presbyterian Church. The seminary is closed, the property is sold off to developers, the dead Passionists were disinterred and buried somewhere else. I don't know what happened to the Stations of the Cross. I still drive by the place from time to time. The word for it is desolation, and it breaks my heart.

Please do not misunderstand. Archie Dinoia has not given up on the Church. He has no truck with self-styled "traditionalists" who claim that only the Tridentine Mass is valid, or with the followers of Marcel Lefebvre in the Society of St. Pius X who claim that the Second Vatican Council was heretical, or with the "sedevacantists" (from "empty chair") who claim the Pope is an imposter. Far from it. "Whether our way of being Catholic before the Council was better, I don't know," says Archie.

The jury is still out. Maybe a century from now a better judgment will be possible. But the initial results are not encouraging. Just think: reduced Mass attendance, seminaries closed or hanging on by their fingertips, a huge defection of priests and nuns, widespread indifference to directives from Rome, sexual scandals, a sense of sin and grace replaced by self-esteem. You want me to go on? I know the Church is not static and is not supposed to be. A religion professor in college used to repeatedly say that the Church is "eschatological," with the accent on all six syllables. We made fun of him, but he was right about that. So we have to look at these last fifty years as a time of trial and error, of reform and, maybe now, reform of reform. But it will be a long time before the Church is again as unconditionally loved, revered, trusted, and depended on the way it was in the first half of the twentieth century. That's about all I have to say.

It is important that he says it, and it is important that we hear it.

An Excursus

Archie Dinoia would fit almost everybody's notion of a conservative. His conservatism may be irritable at times, but it is not angry. He understands that Catholicism is very large, and much larger from the inside than from the outside. I don't think he wants to kick anybody out, although he wishes it were more generally understood what is entailed in being in. I am not original in adopting James Joyce's observation that the Catholic Church is "Here Comes Everybody." I have used the expression on many occasions. Although Joyce was no expert on ecclesiology and not even a very good Catholic, "Here Comes Everybody" catches something important about Catholicism. Were the word not so debased in contemporary chatter, one might say it underscores the "inclusiveness" of the Church. The better image is that of a mother reaching out to embrace all her children.

I have, however, been challenged on whether Joyce did in fact say that the Church is Here Comes Everybody. I am grateful to readers of *First Things* who have come to my support. Particularly helpful is a reflection from Craig Payne of Indian Hills College in Ottumwa, Iowa. Is it possible that what was not seen by scholars in the Ivy League has been revealed to Indian Hills? Mr. Payne suggests that the text of *Finnegans Wake* supports the application of H.C.E. to the Catholic (and particularly the Irish Catholic) Church. His report is submitted in evidence:

In the ongoing dream of Mr. Porter, Porter's dream persona, Humphrey Chimpden Earwicker (HCE), appears to have become identified at one point with Finn MacCool, the legendary or semilegendary Irish hero of the third century A.D., leader of the Fianna warriors. MacCool is partly human and partly divine; in later stories, he is also described as being of gigantic stature. Anyway—during this sequence the following passages occur:

"The great fact emerges that after that historic date all holographs so far exhumed initialled by Haromphry bear the sigla H.C.E. and while he was only and long and always good Dook Umphrey for the hunger–lean spalpeens of Lucalizod and Chimbers to his cronies it was equally certainly a pleasant turn of the populace which gave him as sense of those normative letters the nickname Here Comes Everybody. An imposing everybody he always indeed looked, constantly the same as and equal to himself and magnificently well worthy of

any and all such universalisation. . . . [F]rom good start to happy finish the truly catholic assemblage gathered together in that king's treat house of satin a lustrelike above floats and footlights . . . in a command performance by special request with the courteous permission for pious purposes the homedromed and enliventh performance of the problem passion play of the millentury, running strong since creation, A Royal Divorce . . . "

A few lines later comes a reference to "the christlikeness of the big cleanminded giant H. C. Earwicker throughout his excellency long vicefreegal existence . . . " "Here Comes Everybody," then, is the other partly human and partly divine Irish giant, the universal and "truly catholic" assemblage, gathered "for pious purposes" to watch yet another performance of a passion play, a play which has run ever since creation, when the "Royal Divorce" took place. And one more point: This passage is presented at precisely the point where the "christlikeness of the big clean-minded giant" HCE is called into serious question, by accusations of sexual misconduct involving himself and a youngster (a girl, in this case). I'm pretty sure this will clear up nothing, as is the case with most Joyceana. However, it was worth a try.

It was, I think, more than a worth a try. It may not be the find of the millentury, but my hunch is that Mr. Payne has hit pay dirt with respect to the ecclesiological significance of H.C.E.

So I'll continue to insist that the Catholic Church is Here Comes Everybody. Like all good mothers, she is forgiving and promiscuous in the reach of her embrace. The only requirement is that we acknowledge our need, that we know we are sinners; sinners forgiven and sinners called to be saints, but sinners nonetheless. If in these pages the gimlet-eyed reader were to detect, here or there, a hint of polemic or a suggestion that some Catholics need to rethink what it means to be Catholic, let it in no way detract from the truth that the Church is Here Comes Everybody. Having been so generously received by the Church, I am in no position to suggest that anybody be excluded. That those authorized to do so are occasionally obliged to put people on notice that they are excluding themselves is quite another matter.

6 | Proposing the Story of the World

But enough, and perhaps more than enough, about what went wrong following the Council. In the 2,000 years of the Church's history, the last 40 may in many ways be viewed as a rough spot. There have been many rougher. This is neither the best of times nor the worst of times but only the brief time of the testing of our fidelity. Much Catholic literature of a traditionalist bent is prone to the sin of morose delectation—dwelling on, and taking delight in, what is wrong. The object of morose delectation is, of course, almost always what others have done wrong. On many matters it is true that what once was is no longer and will not be again. That is the way it is with history, including the history of the Church. What Augustine called the City of God is, like the earthly city, a creature of time. Unlike the earthly city, its destination is eternal life, the New Jerusalem. That is the tradition, the truth that is passed on from generation to generation. The oft-quoted words of Jaroslav Pelikan are in order: "Tradition is the living faith of the dead;

traditionalism is the dead faith of the living. Tradition lives in conversation with the past, while remembering where we are and when we are and that it is we who have to decide."

There is the great danger of showing disrespect for what has gone before. Much of the innovation and reckless experimentation following the Council fell prey to that danger. There is also the danger of idealizing and attempting to calcify what used to be. Some, as we have seen, have drawn up a balance sheet of pluses and minuses since the Council. For those who assume that change is good and the more change the better, that is a senseless exercise. For such people, there are only pluses. For those who view change with suspicion yet try to be fair, a balance sheet seems almost unavoidable. Concerning institutional strength, communal cohesion and vitality, and the everyday practice of the faith in family and parish life, such balance sheets frequently arrive at a grim conclusion: The consequences of the Council have been disastrous. Some keepers of the ledgers draw a further conclusion: *post hoc ergo propter hoc*—after which, therefore because of which. The conclusion is that what has happened after the Council happened because of the Council. That conclusion may be on the cusp of heresy, implying that the Council was not under the guidance of the Holy Spirit, and it is not becoming for self-defined guardians of orthodoxy to flirt with heresy.

I suppose that nobody can offer an entirely "balanced" assessment of what has happened, and I have already indicated some of my own conclusions. In drawing up a balance sheet, 1960 seems like the logical baseline. It was before the Council and just when all the indices of Catholic vitality were at their peak. In addition, Catholics were "coming of age" in America, and Catholicism was being not only accepted but cele-brated by the wider culture. There was JFK of course, and, somewhat earlier, movies such as *The Bells of St. Mary's*, with Bing Crosby and Ingrid Bergman; or *The Song of Bernadette*, a sympathetic telling of the miracle of Lourdes, with Jennifer Jones and Charles Bickford. In 1987, I published a book, *The Catholic Moment*, explaining why the Catholic Church is the "lead community" in advancing most of what we should hope for in the Church and the world. About the same time, Pat Buchanan, the conservative columnist and erstwhile presiden-tial candidate, published *Right from the Start*, a fond remembrance of growing up Catholic and Irish in the 1940s and 1950s. I knew Buchanan casually and he sent me a copy of his book inscribed with this: "I too believe in the Catholic Moment. It was about forty years ago and is not likely to hap-pen again." Touché.

But was the state of Catholic music and liturgy, for instance, better in 1960 than it is today? There were the hurried Masses mumbled in Latin, the congregation mostly a silent audience "attending" what was referred to as "Father McCormick's Mass." That is what the earlier liturgical movement wanted to replace with what the Council called the full, conscious, and ac-tive participation of the people. Was the sometimes slapdash mumbling more the norm in 1960 than the chat show, or the hand-clapping sing-along, was the norm in, say, 1985? The question can probably not be answered without a clear record of what was happening in the 20,000 parishes around the country. If one reads old issues of *Orate Fratres* complaining about how the Mass was done prior to the Council alongside current issues of *The Latin Mass* complaining about how the Mass is done now, one gets a strikingly similar impression of liturgical travesties. My hunch is that in 1960 there was a deeper sense of the mystery of what God was doing at and around the altar. Quite apart from our sense of it, God was doing the same thing in 1985 that He was doing in 1960 or, for that matter, when Our Lord instituted the Eucharist in the Upper Room. And, as I said earlier, the postconciliar liturgical silly season is past or passing. All who have been paying attention know that today's younger priests and seminarians are determined to celebrate the rite of the Novus Ordo with reverence and even solemnity.

Those who draw up such balance sheets may respond that that may well be, but the truth is that in 1960 80 percent of self-identified Catholics went to Mass every week; today, the figure is, at most, 50 percent and probably closer to 30. It is hard to argue that that is not a clear negative. And yet, given that since the Council almost two generations have gone un-catechized, given the culturally reinforced orthodoxy that rules are out and individual choice is in, and given decades of sustained assault on magisterial teaching by theologians and priests of "the post–Vatican II Church," it seems to me re-markable that 30-plus percent of Catholics go to Mass once a week or more. Almost twice that number claim to go once a month and consider themselves to be "good Catholics," which is understandable in view of what they have been mistaught what it means to be a good Catholic. This is hardly a small remnant. Some conservatives say we should stop deceiving ourselves. There are not, they say, 65 million Catholics in the United States but, at the most, 20 or even 10 million. That is a Protestant way of thinking, and I decline to go along with it. I did not become a Catholic in order to be a Protestant.

Once a Catholic always a Catholic, or so it is said. A good many of those who are called, or call themselves, lapsed Catholics, whether they are lapsed by virtue of sloth or doubt, or morally disordered lives, still hang around the Catholic Thing. The Catholic sensibility is to encourage them to hang around. Remember "Here Comes Everybody." C. S. Lewis was not a Catholic but in this respect he evidenced a Catholic sensibility. He wrote:

A man who disbelieved the Christian story as fact but continually fed on it as myth would, perhaps, be more spiritually alive than one who assented and did not think much about it. The modernist—the extreme modernist, infidel in all but name—need not be called a fool or hypocrite because he obstinately retains, even in the midst of his intellectual atheism, the language, rites, sacraments, and story of the Christians. The poor man may be clinging (with a wisdom he himself by no means understands) to that which is his life.

There is a vast pool of such Catholics today. They should be encouraged. They are the reason why the Church, very much including the voices of John Paul the Great and Benedict XVI, so urgently call for re-evangelization. And, for many, not re-catechesis but catechesis for the first time.

On the plus side of the balance sheet, it seems likely that many more Catholics today are reading and studying the Bible. It is not true, as some Protestant polemics would have it, that Catholics were forbidden to read the Bible before the Council. But many did not see the point of it, since they could consult church teaching to find out what the Bible *really* means. The Council's constitution on Scripture, *Dei Verbum* (The Word of God), "earnestly and specifically urges all the Christian faithful, especially religious, to learn by frequent reading of the divine Scriptures the 'excelling knowledge of Jesus Christ' (Philippians 3)." The Council quotes St. Jerome: "Ignorance of the Scriptures is ignorance of Christ." "Therefore," the Council said, "they should gladly put themselves in touch with the sacred text itself, whether it be through the liturgy, rich in the divine word, or through devotional readings, or through instructions suitable for the purpose and other aids which in our time are commendably available everywhere." Bible study and study groups are today commendably available everywhere. Well, almost everywhere.

This, too, is part of *ressourcement*, of returning to the sources, in a way that helps Catholics to think with the Church *(sentire cum ecclesia)* as the Church draws upon and authoritatively interprets the sacred text. And in personal and group study Catholics are not limited to the lamentably clunky translation that is the New American Bible (regrettably, the translation to which Catholics are subjected at Mass). Is there the danger that studying the Bible will, in a Protestant fashion, lead Catholics to pit their personal interpretation against magisterial teaching? (In this they would be following the bad example set by too many Catholic biblical scholars.) Of course that is a danger. But the alternative is to be ignorant of the Bible. Studying the Bible, as the study of any great text, raises questions. But one questions in order to understand. Again, thinking with the Church begins with thinking.

In an encyclical on evangelization, *Redemptoris Missio*, John Paul the Great offered a marvelous formulation: The Church imposes nothing, she only proposes. What she proposes, however, is the truth, and the truth does impose itself. That is because, at least according to Catholic anthropology, human beings are, so to speak, hard-wired for the truth. We live in an intelligible world that is accessible to reason. Our mind participates in the mind of God. With respect to the right ordering of our lives and the right ordering of the world, we can know God's law. Here, too, St. Thomas Aquinas is the helpful teacher. He writes of four distinct meanings of law: There is the eternal law, the natural law, the positive law, and the divine law. The eternal law is one with the eternal Being of God Himself. The natural law—and here Thomas follows St. Paul in Romans 1 and 2—is the understanding of right and wrong that is written on every human heart. These are the truths that we "cannot not know," although we can deny that we know them and live as though we do not know them. The positive law is human law: the man-made laws and regulations that societies adopt. These may or may not be in agreement with eternal and natural law. Fourth and finally, there is divine law, the law and laws revealed by God in the Scriptures and Spirit-guided teaching of the Church.

There is no denying that this way of thinking about law and the right ordering of the world—and especially the right ordering of our own lives!—goes against the grain of our culture. The very idea of "moral truth" is a puzzlement and offense to many of our contemporaries. Twenty-five years ago the philosopher Alasdair MacIntyre published his extraordinary little book, *After Virtue*. His argument, put much too simply, is that not only intellectuals but our popular culture has largely abandoned an understanding of moral truth and virtue, with the result that we are all dog-paddling in the murky sea of "modern emotivism."

Morality has become almost totally a matter of feelings and preferences. You have yours and I have mine. If I say that something is "wrong," I am expressing no more than my personal preference. "I am not comfortable with that." "I feel that is not right." "I would prefer you not do that." In short, the making of arguments is replaced by the expression of emotions. In such a cultural context, the appeal to "conscience" is only an appeal to my personal preference. Conscience, in this view, does not discern moral truth but subjectively establishes the truth. This deep shift in the understanding of conscience and truth is addressed in the 1993 encyclical of John Paul II, *Veritatis Splendor* (The Splendor of Truth). An extended quotation is in order:

> *Certain currents of modern thought have gone so far as to exalt freedom to such an extent that it becomes an absolute, which would then be the source of values. This is the direction taken by doctrines which have lost the sense of the transcendent or which are explicitly atheist. The individual conscience is accorded the status of a supreme tribunal of moral judgment which hands down categorical and infallible decisions about good and evil. To the affirmation that one has a duty to follow one's conscience is unduly added the affirmation that one's moral judgment is true merely by the fact that it has its origin in the conscience. But in this way the inescapable claims of truth disappear, yielding their place to a criterion of sincerity, authenticity and "being at peace with oneself", so much so that some have come to adopt a radically subjectivistic conception of moral judgment.*

*As is immediately evident, the crisis [...]
unconnected with this development. Once [...]
universal truth about the good, knowable by h[...]
lost, inevitably the notion of conscience also cha[...]
is no longer considered in its primordial reali[...]
person's intelligence, the function of which is to apply the
universal knowledge of the good in a specific situation and thus
to express a judgment about the right conduct to be chosen here
and now. Instead, there is a tendency to grant to the individual
conscience the prerogative of independently determining the
criteria of good and evil and then acting accordingly. Such an
outlook is quite congenial to an individualist ethic, wherein
each individual is faced with his own truth, different from the
truth of others. Taken to its extreme consequences, this
individualism leads to a denial of the very idea of human
nature.*

*These different notions are at the origin of currents of
thought which posit a radical opposition between moral law
and conscience, and between nature and freedom. (Veritatis
Splendor, 32)*

The Church's way of thinking holds that there is such a thing
as moral truth. It is not only in our time that agreement on this
can hardly be taken for granted. Pontius Pilate said, "So you are a
king?" Jesus answered, "You say that I am a king. For this I was
born and for this I came into the world, to bear witness to the
truth. Every one who is of the truth hears my voice." And Pilate
said, "What is truth?" Two thousand years later, many of the
brightest and best in our world deem it the mark of intellectual
sophistication to echo Pilate's question, "What is truth?"

live in the splendor of truth is, by the gifts of nature and grace, to cultivate the virtues that are in accord with the truth. You may well be familiar with the concluding lines of Alasdair MacIntyre's *After Virtue*, for they are often quoted. But in this context they deserve to be recalled once again. He is speaking of the coming ages of barbarity and darkness that, he believes, are replacing an earlier time when civilization at least aspired to truth and virtue. MacIntyre wrote:

> *If my account of our moral condition is correct, we ought also to conclude that for some time now we too have reached that turning point. What matters at this stage is the construction of local forms of community within which civility and the intellectual and moral life can be sustained through the new dark ages which are already upon us. And if the tradition of the virtues was able to survive the horrors of the last dark ages, we are not entirely without grounds for hope. This time, however, the barbarians are not waiting beyond the frontiers; they have already been governing us for quite some time. And it is our lack of consciousness of this that constitutes part of our predicament. We are waiting not for a Godot but for another—doubtless very different—St. Benedict.*

And now, twenty-five years after those words were written, we have Benedict XVI. After he became pope, Joseph Ratzinger explained that he had two figures in mind when he chose his name. Giacomo della Chiesa became Benedict XV shortly after the outbreak of World War I in 1914, and he strove mightily, albeit in vain, to achieve peace between the belligerents. Also, and years before John Paul the Great's mighty exertions in this connection, Benedict XV tried to find a path of reconciliation with the Orthodox churches, which were formally alienated in the eleventh century. To that end he established the Congregation for the Oriental Church and the Pontifical Oriental Institute in Rome. The other figure that Pope Benedict had in mind is the sixth-century St. Benedict, who is known as "the father of Western monasticism." When the former Roman Empire was in shambles, he and his "Rule of St. Benedict" laid the foundation for a movement that preserved and finally rejuvenated the moral, cultural, and intellectual tradition that we rightly revere as Western civilization. Benedict XVI is doubtless a very different Benedict, and we should be more than open to the possibility that he is the Benedict for whom MacIntyre says we have been waiting. A measure of his success will be his ability to persuade the world that "moral truth" is not an oxymoron. We all have a part in that task of persuasion.

The insistence upon moral truth and the conscience as a faculty for discerning truth puts the Catholic way of thinking at odds with the dominant mindset of American culture; this results, perhaps inevitably, in a deep disagreement also among Catholics, some urging a greater accommodation to the surrounding culture and others insisting that the way of fidelity is the way of unapologetic confrontation. The first party is loosely defined as progressive, and the second is just as loosely defined as conservative. There is no doubt that Catholicism, when proposed and lived with integrity, is in tension with our cultural surround. In this sense, Catholicism is countercultural, and many contend that we should not just resign ourselves to that fact but exult in it.

In recent decades, American habits of thought and practice have made deep inroads also in Catholic life. This is evident in an individualism that views the very idea of authority and tradition as an imposition upon the exercise of freedom. The term "pro-choice," so prominent in the abortion controversy, becomes the term of choice for virtually everything. Religious allegiance is a matter of spiritual preference; church doctrine is to be democratically determined or is an offering of options from which we pick and choose (hence the phrase "cafeteria Catholic"—and, following the election of Benedict, the quip, "The cafeteria is closed."); worship is tailored to "meet my needs," and on and on. In resistance to these patterns of thought and practice, Catholicism is indeed countercultural. And yet . . .

The spirit of Catholicism is not countercultural by choice. Faced with opposition, the Church may find herself in a countercultural circumstance by necessity. This is why the Church's liturgical calendar is chockfull of days celebrating the martyrs. No matter how successful, secure, and at home the Church may think she is in a particular culture, the faithful are liturgically alerted to the reality that persecution and martyrdom may be close at hand. John Paul the Great incessantly reminded us that the past century was the century of martyrs; indeed, more people died for the faith in the past century than in all nineteen prior centuries combined. At the deepest level, the Church's self-understanding means that she can never be comfortably and securely settled in any place or period of history short of the fulfillment of her unceasing prayer, "Thy kingdom come."

The second-century Letter to Diognetus describes Christians as "alien citizens" for whom "every foreign country is a homeland and every homeland is a foreign country." St. Augustine speaks of the City of God on pilgrimage through the city of man on the way to the Kingdom. In the third eucharistic prayer, we pray, "Strengthen in faith and love your pilgrim Church on earth." The Church lives "between the times"—between the time of Christ's definitive resurrection victory and the time when the consummation of that victory is evident to all; the time when, as St. Paul says to the Philippians, "[E]very knee shall bow and every tongue confess that Jesus Christ is Lord to the glory of God the Father." And so it is that in her deepest self-understanding the Church maintains a countercultural edge. When that edge is blunted, when it is no longer part of the felt experience of being Catholic, something has gone seriously wrong. And yet . . .

The spirit of Catholicism is not countercultural by choice. The Church may sometimes appear to be against the world, but she is only against the world *for* the world. John 3:16, perhaps the best known of New Testament passages, begins, "God so loved the world . . ." That is immediately followed by: "For God sent the Son into the world not to condemn the world but that the world might be saved through him." The Church is the continuation through time of the mission of Christ and shares his passionate love for the world. The Catholic disposition is culture-affirming. This is the authentic humanism, radical to the point of believing that God has in Christ invested Himself in the *humanum*, in the human project. The Church says with Irenaeus and the early fathers that in the incarnation all has been assumed by Christ that all might be redeemed by Christ. "The glory of God," said Irenaeus, "is man fully alive." The Church imposes nothing; she only proposes, but what a proposal! When that proposal is rejected, the Church is joined with Christ in weeping over the human city that did not know the time of its visitation.

In the arts, in intellectual life, in science and technology, in every aspiration toward excellence, and in the everyday tending to daily needs, the Church is on the side of the human project. Within the history of the Church, there are world-denying traditions of radical denial and asceticism, but these, too, aim to exemplify the gracing of the human capacity to aspire toward and experience in part the transcendent glory of the oncoming Kingdom. The Catholic disposition is well expressed in the familiar maxim of Thomas Aquinas that grace does not destroy nature but fulfills it. Nature, beginning with human nature, is deeply wounded by sin, but it is not, as some Christian thinkers have claimed, totally corrupted or depraved. We read in Genesis, "And God saw everything he had made, and behold it was very good." Despite everything, God has not taken back that judgment. He sent his Son to save the world because the world was worth saving. The Catholic spirit sings with the Psalmist:

> *When I look at your heavens, the*
> *work of your fingers,*
> *the moon and the stars which you*
> *have established;*
> *what is man that you are mindful*
> *of him,*
> *and the son of man that you*
> *care for him?*
> *Yet you have made him little less*
> *than God,*

and you crown him with glory
and honor.
(Psalm 8)

David Tracy, a contemporary theologian, captures something key to the Catholic spirit in his treatment of "the analogical imagination."[1] The analogical imagination seeks out resemblances, similarities, correspondences, and overlapping truths between apparently disparate realities. It aims at synthesis on the far side of experienced antithesis, it aims at likeness on the far side of unlikeness. Thus human sexuality in marriage is like the union between Christ and his bride the Church. Thus, as Vatican II insisted, the Church is not an alternative to the world but is a sacrament for the world, and even of the world. She is that part of the world aspiring to the world's fulfillment in Christ.

By way of contrast to the analogical sensibility is the dialectical sensibility. Here the emphasis is on either/or, on a juxtaposing of contraries, and between them a stark choice is demanded. Here it is nature *or* grace, Church *or* world, reason *or* faith, Christ *or* culture. The dialectical disposition has provided Christian history with moments of spiritual and intellectual pyrotechnics in the likes of Martin Luther and, perhaps above all, Soren Kierkegaard. It is not the Catholic spirit.

If one presses the distinction between the analogical and dialectical too far, the ironic outcome is that the argument for the analogical imagination itself becomes dialectical, demanding a stark either/or. The analogical imagination is precisely that, a matter of imagination, a matter of sensibility. That is why we speak of the spirit of Catholicism rather than the logic of

Catholicism, although Catholicism is also perfectly logical. It is a matter of finding analogies with hope even in a world that denies that hope. The spirit of Catholicism begins with an irrepressible sympathy for the world that is the object of God's love in Christ. It sees in the world ever so much more than the world dares to see in itself. It sees in every human being a potentiality for glory far beyond that person's timorous aspirations. Remember how often John Paul II cited the passage from *Gaudium et Spes* that says Christ is not only the revelation of God to man but the revelation of man to himself. This is what it means to look into the face of your neighbor and see, in the presence of promise, the face of Christ.

To put it simply and boldly, the gospel of Jesus Christ is the story of the world.[2] The great problem is that the world does not know its own story. The gospel of Jesus Christ is not an imposition upon the world but the proposal to the world of its own true story. For the Catholic Christian, the world is not alien territory but a creation of love that has tragically alienated itself from its Creator. The mission of the Church is to call the world home. Consider Luke 10: "And when he drew near and saw the city he wept over it, saying, 'Would that even today you knew the things that make for peace.'" Or Matthew 23: "O Jerusalem, Jerusalem, killing the prophets and stoning those who are sent to you! How often would I have gathered your children together as a hen gathers her brood under her wings, and you would not!"

In the mission of his Church, Christ is inviting, cajoling, urging, wooing—calling the world home to itself. And yes, he warns of the consequences if the call is rejected: A wayward world that rejects the invitation, that prefers darkness to light, and that turns against its own true story in vicious hostility. Yet Christ and his Church are persistent. "Love your enemies," he says. "Do not return evil for evil." Never tire of engaging them, of persuading them, of pointing out in their lives the signals of the transcendent glory for which they were created. Never weary of proposing to them the true story of their lives.

I count it one of the great blessings of my life to have worked closely with Martin Luther King, Jr., especially during the three years before his assassination on April 4, 1968. It is no secret that his personal life was in some ways a moral shambles, but he was nonetheless a prophetic voice. Of him, too, it was true that, in the words of St. Paul, "We have this treasure in earthen vessels to show that the transcendent power belongs to God and not to us." Dr. King was fond of saying, "Whom you would change you must first love, and they must know that you love them." In a sense, that is pretty obvious. Every good parent, every good priest, every good teacher knows it to be true. People, whether young or old, are not likely to take their lead from someone who they think does not have their interests at heart, from someone who does not love them. The Church loves the world, as God in Christ loves the world. As John Paul II teaches us, the Church imposes nothing, she only proposes. As a lover to the beloved she proposes—persistently, persuasively, winsomely, she proposes not an alien truth but the world's own true story.

Remember St. Paul and the Corinthians. We hear people talk about how we should return to the purity and love and harmony of the early Christians. They should read Paul's letters to the Corinthians. The Corinthian Christians were a proud, fractious, and stiff-necked bunch. In the first twelve chapters of I

Corinthians, Paul addresses their many disagreements and quarrels. Finally we come to the last verse of chapter 12, where he says, "I will show you a more excellent way." Then follows the unparalleled hymn of love that is chapter 13:

> *Though I speak in the tongues of men and of angels, but have not love, I am a noisy gong or a clanging cymbal . . .*
>
> *Love is patient and kind; love is not jealous or boastful . . .*
>
> *Love bears all things, believes all things, hopes all things, endures all things . . .*
>
> *Love never ends. As for prophecies, they will pass away; as for tongues, they will cease; as for knowledge, it will pass away. . . .*
>
> *So faith, hope, love abide, these three; but the greatest of these is love.*

That is the proposal that Christ and his Church make to the world: "Let us show you a more excellent way." And if the proposal is rejected, we are braced for that. The worst they can do is kill us. As they killed the one whom we follow, as they killed the martyrs. Every century of fidelity is a century of the martyrs. It is as true of the twenty-first century as it was of the third when Tertullian said, "The blood of the martyrs is the seed of the Church."

Many have noted a difference between John Paul II and Benedict XVI. The former spoke of "a springtime of evangelization." He invited us to see this new century and this new millennium as a time of high promise. The latter, at least in his many writings as Joseph Ratzinger, urged that we brace ourselves for a time of deepened indifference and heightened hostility. Some mistakenly describe this as a difference between optimism and pessimism. But optimism is not a Christian virtue. Optimism is simply a matter of optics, of seeing what one wants to see and not seeing what one does not want to see. Between the two popes is, perhaps, a different reading of our historical moment. But both teach, and all faithful Christians understand, that our hope is not contingent upon the mood of the world in our brief moment in time.

Paul writes to Timothy that he is to proclaim the word "in season and out of season," when it is popular and when it is despised. When I was a boy, I was impressed by how often clergy would cite the promise of Isaiah that "the word will not return empty." I thought that was a passage of consolation for ineffective communicators. As I grew older, I found myself depending upon that passage more and more. Innumerable saints have said in their different ways that the task of the Church is not to be successful but to be faithful. Whether we are on the cusp of a springtime of evangelization or of a return to the contemporary world's version of the catacombs, the word of John Paul and of Benedict, and of all who are faithful, is the word of the resurrected Jesus to his frightened disciples, "Be not afraid."

The story of Jesus Christ is the true story of the world. Not just of the religious world or of the spiritual world but of what we are given to calling the real world. I once spoke at a retreat of a large group of priests in the Midwest and was introduced by the bishop. "We have had two days of reflection on liturgy and sacramental theology," he said, "and I am sure we have all been spiritually strengthened. Now Father Neuhaus will address us on the Church and political responsibility, thus bringing us back to the real world." The real world? It was possibly just a slip of the tongue, but a slip of the tongue may reflect a slip of the mind and a slip of the soul. What is done in liturgy, what is effected in the sacraments, *is* the real world, or else it is no more than delusion. A comforting delusion, a beautiful delusion, an uplifting delusion, but delusion nonetheless. Recall Flannery O'Connor's response when at a Manhattan dinner party the novelist Mary McCarthy was going on about how she had not abandoned her Catholicism altogether. McCarthy allowed that she still found the Mass "a meaningful symbol." To which O'Connor muttered for all to hear, "If it's just a symbol, I say to hell with it."

The gospel of Jesus Christ is what some literary critics call a meta-narrative. It is the story that encompasses all the other stories that we tell about the world, and about ourselves in the world. It is not one more story within the many stories of the world. It is the story of the world, of which all the other stories are part. There are competing meta-narratives. Some of them are proposed by other religions and philosophies. In the century past, millions of people believed, or were told they must believe, in Karl Marx's meta-narrative of dialectical materialism leading to the end of the state and the kingdom of freedom. Meta-narratives can be true or false. There is inescapably an element of faith in committing oneself to a meta-narrative. Jesus said, "I am the way and the truth and the life"—not *a* way, *a* truth, and *a* life. If he is the way, the truth, and the life, he is that for everyone and everything.

Faith commitments are inescapable. This is ably argued by Michael Polanyi in his classic *Personal Knowledge*.[3] Even the most systematically skeptical have no choice but to take many things on faith: In our reliance on what we call the laws of nature, in our dependence upon the reliability of mechanical and technological operations that few of us understand, and, above all, in personal exchanges of every kind, we live by faith. The relentlessly consistent skeptic is ill-prepared for a world of inevitable risks. Moreover, he violates the consistency of his skepticism by not being skeptical about his skepticism. A faith commitment to the doctrine of skepticism produces the meta-narrative that is the chief rival to explicit faith in the modern world, namely, the meta-narrative that there is no narrative. In this view, reality has neither point nor intention nor purpose and we will all depart this world by the same accident by which we arrived. One notes in passing that to speak of "accident" is to assume the existence of something that is not accident, something like purpose, maybe.

These are heavy philosophical questions and I have touched on them in only a cursory fashion. But touch on them we must if we are to understand the nature of the confusion and malaise that afflicts so many Catholics, and not least in North America. For forty years, Catholicism has been assailed by crisis upon crisis. The crisis of sexual ethics, the crisis of priestly vocations, the crisis of collapsing orders of women religious, the sex-abuse crisis, and on and on. It is, I believe, not simplistic to say that they all come down to a crisis of faith. I wrote extensively in *First Things* and elsewhere on the sex-abuse crisis that erupted first in Boston in January 2002. I said the crisis was about three things: fidelity, fidelity, and fidelity. Critics complained that I was greatly oversimplifying the matter. I think not.

It is the simple truth that, if priests and bishops had been faithful to their vows of fidelity, there would have been no sex-abuse crisis. The crisis took a terrifying toll: on teenage boys and young men abused by priests who succumbed to same-sex desires; on priests falsely accused and priests deprived of their ministries on the basis of unjust and unverified suspicions; on the relationships of trust between priests and bishops; and on dioceses that have surrendered to the state their constitutional rights of self-governance. And that is not to mention the payoffs to extortionists and their lawyers that are reliably estimated to amount to more than a billion dollars. It was and is a crisis of many dimensions, but at its heart it is a crisis of faith.

Post hoc ergo propter hoc? Was the Council at fault? No, I don't think so. John Paul the Great was right: Maybe, as he once said, there was an element of "evangelical naïveté" in some of the council documents, but the Council was evangelical through and through. The Spirit guided what the bishops said at the Council, but the Spirit did not show them at the time what would be done with what they said. That would come later. The best and the brightest of those who tutored the bishops at the Council—de Lubac, Balthasar, Congar, Ratzinger—were appalled by what was done with what the Council said. There followed a long way back; it was led hesitantly by Paul VI, with buoyant confidence by John Paul II, and now, with a gentle but firm pastoral hand, it is led by Benedict XVI. It is the long way back to the Council. The great wrong turn after the Council was the disconnecting of *aggiornamento* from *ressourcement*—making the tradition relevant to "the real world" without reappropriating the tradition that throws that world into question. Many Catholic thinkers were satisfied to have the gospel, which is the story of the world, achieve an honorary place among the many other stories of the world. At last, they said, the Church is making its peace with "the real world."

In her engagement with other stories—what are fashionably called other "social constructions of reality"—the pilgrim Church on earth is not unaffected. New questions are raised, old questions are raised in new ways. Jesus promised that he would send the Spirit to lead the Church into the fullness of truth, and the Spirit is leading still. In the nineteenth century, John Henry Newman adumbrated, and in the twentieth century the Church officially embraced, an understanding of "the development of doctrine."[4] Confronted by new challenges, the Church clarifies what was ambiguous, illuminates what was obscure, corrects what was misunderstood, makes explicit what was implicit. The Church does not claim to possess an understanding of the fullness of the truth about everything. She is not embarrassed to admit that she is a creature of history. She is the pilgrim Church, she is the Church on the way. With St. Paul she says, "Now we see in a glass darkly; now we know in part, then we shall know even as we are known."

In Union City, New Jersey, Archie Dinoia was told that there is the "teaching Church" and the "learning Church"—*ecclesia docens* and *ecclesia discens*. The bishop and the pope taught, and everybody else listened and learned. For all practical purposes, the sister in the classroom—backed up by the curate, pastor, bishop, and pope—did the teaching and "the faithful" proved they were faithful by their "docility" in listening and learning. In the usual caricature, the duty of the laity was to pray, pay, and obey. Docility is not a word that, for most people in our culture, comes trippingly to the tongue. It suggests less a Christian virtue than a dumb passivity. But docility is a mark of humility, another unpopular word. Interrupting Winston Churchill in mid-tirade against his successor, Clement Atlee, a colleague of Churchill's said, "But surely you must admit that Mr. Atlee is a humble man." To which Churchill responded, "Mr. Atlee has a great deal to be humble about." To say a person is humble is today not necessarily understood as a compliment.

But it is docility and the virtue of humility that gladly says, "Now we know in part, then we shall know even as we are known." Docility is openness, even eagerness, to learn, knowing that we also learn by being taught. It is not that bishops and popes are necessarily smarter than we are. I know a good many bishops who are ill-educated and slow-witted, and history leaves no doubt that the same could be said of some popes, although not, thank God, in the last couple of hundred years. The teaching authority of bishops and popes, however, finally lies not in their education or intellectual prowess but in their charism. Charism is the gift that attends the office. It is the gift of the Spirit that Jesus promised the apostles, and bishops are the successors to the apostles. Their charism and their fidelity to the tradition they are ordained to transmit is what matters. That is why even the brightest Catholic views even the dimmest bishop as his teacher. Although he may have to help the teacher to teach more truly, a Catholic who does not understand that is missing something essential to being Catholic.

The service of the *ecclesia docens* is the Magisterium of the Church, the bishops with and under the pope, who is Peter among us. But it is no secret that the *ecclesia docens* is also the *ecclesia discens*. Bishops and popes are also learning. The history of the Church is a long learning curve, and the curve will not end until we all "know even as we are known." In the early centuries, the Church was learning through councils such as those at Nicea and Chalcedon how to speak more truly about, for instance, the relationship between the human and divine natures in Christ and the ways in which God is one and yet three. I referred earlier to John Henry Newman's writing about how it was in the fourth century that many bishops had succumbed to Arianism, the heresy denying the full divinity of Christ, but the lay people upheld the orthodox teaching. Scholars today dispute some of the particulars of Newman's account, but there is no denying that the *ecclesia docens* is also the *ecclesia discens*, and can be instructed by the *ecclesia discens*, meaning the laity. This is the legitimate and necessary role of the *consensus fidelium*, which I discussed earlier.

The life of the Church can be understood—not exhaustively but in important part—as a continuing conversation. The Magisterium is the moderator of the conversation and sets the rules, making sure it is a conversation and not a cacophonous brawl. Tradition, said Chesterton, is the democracy of the dead, and the Magisterium assures that, in that sense, the conversation is democratic. The conversation is not about whatever anybody wants to talk about it. It is about, in the words of the New Testament letter of Jude, "the faith once delivered to the saints." This is called "the deposit of faith"—the truth (composed of particular truths) by which the Church is constituted; the revelation of God given in the history of Israel and preeminently in the Christ event and testified to by the divinely inspired Scriptures. In clarifying and making explicit what was implicit, the Magisterium sometimes says different things differently. That is to be expected in a living tradition, in a conversation through time. As we have seen, there are those who jump upon instances of what they insist upon calling "changes" in the tradition, thereby hoping to introduce their preferred changes. Whether we call a magisterial clarification a "change" or a "development" would seem to be no more than a semantic dispute, but a great deal depends upon it.

It is in part a matter of disposition, as in docility. And it is in part a matter of faith, as in "I believe in one, holy, catholic, and apostolic Church." The latter means not only that I believe there is such a Church but that I believe the Church. The Magisterium is by no means the only voice *in* the Church, but it is the authoritative voice *of* the Church. How the many voices in the Church can and do influence the authoritative voice of the Church is, as mentioned earlier, described with great sophistication in the 1990 instruction "The Ecclesial Vocation of the Theologian," which was issued by the Congregation for the Doctrine of the Faith, headed by Joseph Cardinal Ratzinger. I mention that document again because it has been sadly neglected by those who are styled and style themselves "dissidents." If I say I want to think for myself, it may sound as though I want to think by myself, but more likely I have joined a herd of independent minds thinking against the authoritative voice of the Church. Once again, *sentire cum ecclesia*—thinking with the Church—begins with thinking. Theology has been described as *fides quaerens intellectum*—faith in search of understanding. In this sense, every faithful Christian is a theologian trying to think his way more deeply into the faith once delivered to the saints.

Not just sometimes, but at the deepest level, we confess, "I do not understand but I believe." And in believing we understand in a way that, as St. Paul puts it, "surpasses understanding." We are finite, God is infinite. In the twelfth century, St. Anselm wrote,

"God is that greater than which cannot be thought." The Church teaches us how to think and speak rightly about that which cannot be adequately thought or spoken. And it sometimes happens that the Church will muster her full authority and infallibly pronounce on a question in dispute. It is itself infallibly taught that the Church will never require assent to what is false. When the Church speaks infallibily, the faithful Catholic assents with heart and mind. We may not understand the pronouncement, we may think the teaching poorly expressed or inadequately supported by argument, but we obey, remembering that the etymology of obedience is "responsive listening."

We obey because we trust the words of Christ to his apostles and to their successors who are the bishops in union with the bishop of Rome. We obey because the ministry of the Magisterium is the ministry of unity, and unity is part of the truth that Christ wills for his Church. The alternative to obedience is to turn the conversation into a cacophony of Christians making it up as they go along. Obedience does not come easily for there is in all of us the rebellious spirit of John Milton's Satan, who would rather rule in hell than obey in heaven. If we will not have obedience, if we will not abide the self-discipline that is involved in *sentire cum ecclesia*, then we would be well advised to make our acquaintance with the innumerable denominations and sects, or start one of our own.

It is now almost half a century since the Second Vatican Council. Catholics in America have expended entire lifetimes in disputing the meaning of the Council. Talent and energy beyond measure have been devoted to the question of what it means to be an "American Catholic." But surely that is the wrong way of putting the question. The great thing to discover is not what it means to be an American Catholic but what it means to be a Catholic American. One might think the noun is more important than the adjective, but that is not necessarily so. The adjective qualifies and, in qualifying, controls. To say I want to be an American Catholic assumes that I know what it means to be an American but am uncertain about the Catholic part of "American Catholic." The goal, rather, is to be a Catholic American; to be a person who knows what it means to be Catholic and is working on what it means to be a Catholic in America.

We hope that being Catholic and being American are compatible, even mutually reinforcing. And most of the time that may be so. But, in the event of conflict, there should be no doubt in my mind that my identity as a Catholic takes priority. After all, it is the Church that embodies the story of the world, including the story of America. The American story is part of the Catholic story, and not the other way around. The Catholic story is the story of Christ, Lord of all, in his Church most fully and rightly ordered and enacted through time. This is not to deny that the lordship of Christ is enacted and asserted by other Christian communities. But again, if the Catholic Church is what she claims to be, she is the gravitational center for all who confess Jesus Christ as Lord. Not incidentally, a robust and uncompromised Catholic identity is not the enemy of ecumenism but the foundation of ecumenism.

The eminent historian John Lukacs, addressing the American Catholic Historical Association, notes that "most American Catholics, certainly during the last hundred years at least, have considered themselves to be Americans who happen to be

Catholic rather than Catholics who happen to be Americans."[5] The "American Catholic" accommodates being Catholic to being American, whereas for the "Catholic American" it is the other way around. Lukacs and many others have traced the historical path of accommodation by which immigrants—among them Irish Americans, German Americans, Polish Americans, and Italian Americans—came to be Americans who happen to be Catholic rather than Catholics who happen to be Americans. In truth, the nineteenth-century immigrants might have identified themselves more strongly with their home country than with being Catholic. Studies suggest that many Poles, Germans, and Italians became more Catholic in America than they had been back home. This was itself, some scholars claim, an accommodation to American culture in which having a definite religious identity was a necessary component of being authentically American.

The story of Catholics and their "coming of age" in America is composed of many parts. Am I urging that the 65 million Catholics in America undo that complicated immigrant story and become "Catholics who happen to be Americans"? Yes and no. As far as history and social dynamics are concerned, there is no way of reversing the story line. In pastoral leadership, catechesis, and spiritual formation, however, it is possible and necessary to present the Church as a distinct society of primary allegiance. Perhaps the majority of Catholics will continue to think of themselves as Americans who happen to be Catholic, but at least the Church will present herself as a "contrast society." In doing so, she will engage many Catholics in the right ordering of their loves and loyalties, and others will at least be alerted to the necessary tension between being Catholic and being American. That tension is to be welcomed and nurtured as a sign of spiritual vitality. Not incidentally—but also not most importantly—that tension will contribute to the spiritual and moral vitality of American society.

Not every Catholic will live in such constructive tension. Far from it. But many will, and it is a source of great encouragement today that so many young people are discovering the high adventure of living in the fullness of the faith. They are, if you will, postmodernist. At the time of the Council and in the years immediately following, the question that agitated so many was how the Church might come to terms with the modern world. In the way the question was too often posed, it was the modern world that was setting the terms. Many young people today are not so impressed with the modern world. They did not emerge from a Catholic "ghetto"; they have lived all their lives with modernity and, although not rejecting it, they have experienced its limitations, its emptiness, its sterility. They are looking for an alternative and are discovering that alternative in the contrast society that is the Catholic Church.

Then, too, there are the younger priests and seminarians, and new orders of monks and nuns who today are flooded with applicants. One thinks of the Franciscan Friars of the Renewal in New York City and the Benedictines of Clear Creek, Oklahoma, and orders of female religious such as the Dominicans of Nashville, Tennessee, the Sisters of Mercy of Alma, Michigan, the Sisters of Life in New York, as well as the many renewal movements such as Focolare, Regnum Christi, the Neocatechumenal Way, the Legionaries of Christ, Opus Dei, and Communion and Liberation. In centuries past, when the Church was in the doldrums, when indifference and corruption were widespread, renewal came from monastic movements and dedicated communities of lay people. That was so in the sixth century with Benedict of Nursia, "the father of Western monasticism," and with the Franciscans, Dominicans, and others centuries later. It may be happening now. Benedict XVI makes no secret of having had this in mind when he chose the name Benedict. The Church began small and is renewed from small beginnings, Pope Benedict has said on many occasions.

Great fires of the Spirit begin with a tiny spark, and now there are many sparks breaking into flames of authentic renewal. "Let the Church be the Church." That was the motto of the mainly Protestant ecumenical movement in the twentieth century. That movement has now come upon hard days, largely because the motto was not put into practice. Soon it was replaced by another motto, "The world sets the agenda for the Church," and Christian faith was dissipated in subservience to alien causes. The Catholic renewal movements of our time are again saying, "Let the Church be the Church." And this time it may happen.

In the 1760s, in the age of Enlightenment, Clement XIII refused the demand of the French government that the Jesuits in France be "nationalized." He insisted that the Society of Jesus continue in the service of the papacy and the universal Church. Clement declared: *Aut sint ut sunt aut non sint*—"Let them be as they are or let them not be at all." What good is the salt if it has lost its savor? One commentator suggests that Pope Benedict might add another clause, *aut non erit*—if the Church is not the Church it *will not* be at all. But of course the Church will always be until the end of time. We have Our Lord's word on that. The question is whether her life *in our time* will be indifferent, fearful, and corrupt or a luminous proposal to the world of a more excellent way. The answer in our time, as so often in the past, may depend upon small communities that mirror to the world the light that came into the world, the light that has not and will never, never ever, be extinguished.[6]

For such intentional communities and for many other Catholics, the tension with the culture will at times be not tension but conflict. Again, the Church does not seek to be countercultural but, when she is countered by the culture, she has no choice but to be countercultural. Or think of it this way: If the culture of the Church—her teachings, practices, and habits of thought—is the culture that comprehends all reality, then it is not a matter of the Church's being countercultural but of the world's being countercultural in challenging the meta-culture of which it is part. This is an audacious, some would say outrageously audacious, way of putting things. But it is an audacity that is inescapably implicit in saying that Jesus Christ is Lord, and he is Lord of all or he is Lord not at all. The *totus Christus* is Christ and his body the Church, and therefore our audacious claim for Christ necessarily entails an audacious claim for his Church.

There is much in what is called the religious culture of America that runs counter to the Catholic way of being Christian. America continues to be in important ways a very Protestant society. American individualism, which is no doubt a source of economic and other strengths, turns religion, too, into a matter of consumer choice and spiritual marketing. As a result, the church (lower case) is understood in terms that are organizational rather than organic. One's church is an association of the like-minded rather than the Mystical Body of Christ gathered in wondrously catholic diversity by the Real Presence. For the Catholic, the "pilgrim Church on earth" is a distinct society of primary allegiance. For the Protestant, one's church is an associational choice based on preferences in morality, teaching, leadership style, or aesthetic taste. For the Protestant, one's church is chosen; the Catholic belongs to the Church because he is among the chosen. He chooses what he is going to do about being chosen, but being chosen is prior to his choosing. He does not join the Church; he belongs to the Church.

These are generalizations about the differences between the Protestant and the Catholic ways of being Christian, but they are, I believe, generalizations that are generally true. Because Protestantism has a thin ecclesiology (doctrine of the Church), it is prone to conflating the Church with the surrounding culture. In some longstanding Protestant understandings of "Christian America," the nation comes perilously close to taking the place of the Church. "Christian America" becomes the community of primary identity and allegiance. Historically, Catholicism frequently had to contend against the formation of national churches. Gallicanism in France and Josephinism in eighteenth-century Austria are notable instances. The more recent history of disputes over what it means to be an American Catholic is yet another instance.

In this light we can understand Joseph Ratzinger's frequent warnings against the dangers of inflating the authority of national episcopal conferences in a way that could encourage the notion of national or regional churches only loosely associated within the one Catholic Church. Some describe this concern as a power contest between Rome and the national bishops conference, and only the naïve would deny that questions of power are involved. Much more importantly at stake, however, is the Church's understanding of herself as a universal and distinct society that cannot be taken captive by any of the "principalities and powers" (St. Paul) of the present age. As Cardinal Ratzinger pressed these questions in the past, so Benedict XVI may be expected to press them in the years ahead.

The more radical proponents of a distinctly American Catholicism advocate a democratizing of the governance of the Church, including the popular election of bishops and parish pastors who, some suggest, would have to stand for reelection after a set term. They favor, inter alia, the ordination of women, married priests, and a relaxation of the Church's teaching on contraception, divorce, and homosexuality. These and other changes, they say, are part of the *aggiornamento* mandated by the spirit, if not the letter, of Vatican II. In response to a proposal such as the ordination of women, the Magisterium says the Church is not authorized to break so radically from the received tradition. To which the proponents say that the people who *are* the Church possess the authority to re-form the Church as they think best.

Again, democracy means that sovereign authority resides in the *demos*, the people. In this connection, Vatican II's frequent reference to the Church as "the People of God" has been exploited to create endless mischief. In the conciliar documents, the People of God refers to the covenant people of Israel continuing as "the light to the world"—*Lumen Gentium*, which is the title of the Council's constitution on the Church—in the one, holy, catholic, and apostolic Church. The champions of an American Catholicism, however, understand the People of God to be the virtual equivalent of democracy's claim to sovereignty, as in the phrase "We the People." Thus they say, "We are the Church"—or, more commonly and for some unexplained reason, dropping the definite article, "We are Church."

All the baptized are part of the Church, are incorporated into the Church, are members of the Body, but neither individually nor collectively do we constitute the Church. Without me and my like-minded friends, the Church is still the Church. The Body is the Body of Christ in which authority is apostolically ordered in the community of bishops in communion with Peter, and in which Christ alone is sovereign. These are the questions at stake in the sometimes arcane discussions of *communio* theology. At an Extraordinary Synod in Rome in 1985, it was declared that *communio* is the key to understanding the Council's teaching on the nature of the Church. Here again one observes that the most lasting contribution of the pontificate of John Paul the Great may be that it gave us the interpretive key, or hermeneutic, for understanding the Council. The Church participates in nothing less than the very community, or *communio*, of God who is Father, Son, and Holy Spirit. (Although the English word "community" can hardly bear the full weight and depth of what is intended by *communio*.)

This is an unabashedly theological, even mystical, way of understanding the Church. It in no way excludes the very human, historical, and even sociological ways of thinking about the Church. After all, we are not ecclesiological docetists. Docetism was an early (and ever recurring) heresy that Christ did not really have a human body, that he did not really suffer and die on the cross. Ecclesiological docetism is to view the Church as a theological abstraction that remains aloof from the very human messiness of history. As important as it is, however, to understand the "pilgrim Church on earth" in earthly and even earthy terms, she remains always and primarily the temporal *communio* with the eternal life of the triune God; she is that part of history which, by virtue of the incarnation in which God becomes man, guides and impels humanity's pilgrimage toward our transcendent destiny. She is the prolepsis—the present anticipation—of the fulfillment of the story of the world. If that is not, above all, how we understand the Church, it is not evident that the Church has a major claim on our attention, never mind our allegiance, at all.

7 | The Center Holds

Is it more than a rhetorical ploy to say that the center holds? After all, people who take a position generally like to claim that their position constitutes the center. Having taken a stand at the center, one then defines the "extremes," usually described as left and right, liberal and conservative. To be sure, there are minorities who gladly identify themselves as being out of the mainstream and do not blanch at being called extreme. They style themselves as revolutionaries or reactionaries, the avant garde or defenders of the ancien régime. But, as I say, they are a minority. For purposes of persuading others, and usually by conviction, most of us are inclined to present our position as considered, thoughtful, and moderate. Our moderation is certified by our making clear beyond doubt that we eschew this extreme, on the one hand, and that extreme, on the other. *Le centre c'est moi!*

At the same time, we want it understood that ours is not the Laodicean center of Revelation 3. Remember the Lord's reproach of the Church in Laodicea: "I know your works; you are neither cold nor hot. Would that you were cold or hot. . . . I will spew you out of my mouth." No, our center is—to borrow Arthur Schlesinger, Jr.'s phrase with reference to American politics—the *vital center*. Conservatives insist that their adherence to magisterial teaching is a *vibrant* orthodoxy, while liberals describe their dissent as being critically *creative*. Please, do not describe my position as hot, in the sense of overheated or fanatical. But neither is it cold, in the sense of conventional or unfeeling. It is warm, as in welcoming. It is cool, as in composed and unruffled. Tired of the contentiousness of extremes in conflict? Welcome to the center.

Once upon a time, before the Second Vatican Council, there were "good Catholics" and "bad Catholics," but everybody knew, or thought they knew, what it meant to be a Catholic. Then, quite suddenly, it seemed that everything was up for grabs, and in the resulting confusions contesting parties vied for the treasured turf called the center. On the left and on the right, people claimed to be "beyond" the old categories of left and right, liberal and conservative. These were the beyondists, and they are with us still. They are usually liberals running away from the sour smell that is liberalism far beyond its sell-by date. And beyondists are sometimes conservatives wanting to distance themselves from the stereotypes of conservatism. Each side typically represents only more of what they say they are beyond. The language of beyondism has to do not with substance but with salesmanship. Beyondism keeps returning us to where the arguments began.

> *I often think it's comical*
> *How nature always does contrive*

That every boy and every gal,
That's born into the world alive,
Is either a little Liberal,
Or else a little Conservative!

W. S. Gilbert didn't have it quite right. We may not be born one way or the other, but having reached the point of taking sides, few of us move beyond it. Yes, it is true that in the 1960s I was viewed as a liberal, but I was a liberal for conservative reasons. When over a long time it was made clear to me that my position was untenable (I will not bore you with the details, but it had to do most importantly with the division of the house over abortion), I did not move beyond liberal and conservative. I became a conservative, or at least what some persist in calling a neoconservative. There comes a time, as the essayist Midge Decter once put it, when one must take the side he is on. If someone proposes to you a position that is beyond left and right, you can be almost certain he's peddling a gussied-up liberalism or gussied-up conservatism. Beyondism is a shell game.

Disputes in the Church are different from disputes in the arena of secular politics, although not so different as one might like to think. I venture the suggestion, that, in trying to understand the intra-Catholic disputes of the years since the Council, it is more helpful to think of two parties: the party of discontinuity and the party of continuity. I venture this proposal in full awareness of E. M. Forster's quip that there are two kinds of people in the world: those who say there are two kinds of people in the world and those who don't. Then there are those who are intimidated by Forster's quip and those who aren't. I'm one of the latter.

And so, allowing for the prescribed nuances, exceptions, and complexities, there is the party of discontinuity and the party of continuity. The party of discontinuity has right-wing and left-wing branches, but they are united in their agreement that the Second Vatican Council was a decisive break in the story of the Catholic Church. The one sees the Council as deviation, or even apostasy; the other sees the Council as liberation, or even revolution. Both see the Council as a break from what had gone before; both speak as if two churches existed, a pre–Vatican II Church and a post–Vatican II Church. Both parties are highly critical of the Church's leadership and had little use for the pontificate of John Paul the Great—the one because he failed to restore what was, the other because he supposedly tried to do just that. These are the two branches of the party of discontinuity. I admit that the term is a bit clumsy, but we might call them the discontinuants.

The rightists in the party of discontinuity are most graphically represented by the late Marcel Lefebvre, a French archbishop, and his followers. Having participated in the Council as a bishop, Lefebvre came to the conviction that the Council was heretical and he went into schism, being excommunicated, after Rome's most arduous efforts to avoid a final break, in 1988. Lefebvrists in the Society of St. Pius X are to be found around the world, and have their American headquarters in Kansas City. Some on the right of the party of discontinuity are "sedevacantists"—from *sede vacante*, meaning "the see is vacant." They believe John Paul II was an imposter, as was Paul VI before him and Benedict XVI after him. They have photos showing that the left earlobe of Giovanni Battista Montini is different from the left earlobe shown in photos of Paul VI, or something like that. In the twilight zones of the Internet, sede-vacantism is conveniently linked to websites about Elvis sightings.

Other discontinuants of a rightist bent are usually not so radical in their views. They include people who say, *sotto voce*, that Vatican II was a mistake; some think it was a catastrophe, others a wrong turn, and yet others a severe bump in the road. They say such things *sotto voce* because the Catholicism they want to repristinate provides no doctrinal resources to justify the claim that Vatican II was simply illegitimate. In their view, the Council was, at the very least, unnecessary. Two councils were quite enough: Trent in the sixteenth century to rebut definitively the Protestant heretics, and Vatican I in the nineteenth century to declare papal infallibility, which would then be sufficient for dealing with all future contingencies. John XXIII's decision to call a council, they believe, was not an inspiration but a wild impulse that a wiser man would have stifled. Discontinuants of the right generally stay in the Church—there being nowhere to go except into the Lefebvre Land of schism—but not without a steady rumbling of complaint.

Representative is a recent column by Pat Buchanan, for whom Vatican II was somewhere between catastrophe and wrong turn. He lists all the things that have gone wrong in the Church since the Council, and it is an impressive list indeed. I mentioned earlier that, in 1987, when I published *The Catholic Moment*, Mr. Buchanan sent me a copy of a book he had just published with the inscription, "I too believe in the Catholic moment. It was forty years ago and is not likely to happen again." That earlier Catholic moment, as he says, was one of full seminaries and full convents, of a burgeoning system of

health care and schools, of colleges and universities intellectu-
ally committed to Catholic truth, of crowded pews, big families,
and a church celebrated by Hollywood and the world to the
ringing of *The Bells of St. Mary's*. Witness now a church dispirited and divided, riddled by scandal, and led by bishops who, if
they are not on the edge of resigning in disgrace, are sheepishly
employed in giving depositions, trying to explain why they
didn't do what they should have done about their clerical
friends who had a penchant for doing rude things with teenaged
boys.

Buchanan's depiction is grim, so grim as to be a caricature.
As also, many will protest, is his depiction of the good old days
too glowing. But caricatures that carry weight with many
thoughtful people are not woven out of whole cloth. In his critique of the Council, Buchanan and many others commit the
fallacy of *post hoc ergo propter hoc*—it happened after the Council,
therefore it happened because of the Council. But the Council
was not responsible for John F. Kennedy and the doctrine he
promulgated in 1960 to the Baptist ministers of Houston that a
Catholic in public life should be indifferent to the teachings of
the Church. The Council did not produce "the sixties," although it did "open the Church's windows to the world" just
when the world was going crazy. An intriguing "what if" exercise is to ask what would have happened if the Council had been
held ten years earlier.

I am convinced that the discontinuants of the right are
wrong to blame the Council. To say that a council is infallible,
which it is, is not to say that a council is omniscient, which it
isn't. In subsequent years, a good many Council fathers have
made no secret of their wish that some documents had been

worded differently so that misunderstanding and deliberate misconstrual could have been avoided. But the responsibility for what has gone wrong—and much has gone wrong, along with much that has gone right—rests, for the most part, with the discontinuants of the left.

Think about it. For forty years, the leftist branch of the party of discontinuity has been agitating the same old issues, all of which come down to sex, power, and freedom (the last understood as license). They have been at it for so long that their cause has the status of a tradition, of which they are the traditionalists. Originally fired by memories of the real or imagined oppressions and constrictions of the "pre–Vatican II Church," in their senescence they grumble about "conservative" younger Catholics, including younger priests, who were inspired by John Paul the Great and the challenge of living the high adventure of a Catholicism freshly discovered and two generations removed from the bitter quarrels between the Pat Buchanans and Father Richard McBriens about whether the years before the Council were the good old days or the bad old days. The traditionalists of the discontinuant left keep scratching the same old sores.

First there was contraception, and with the orchestrated assault on the 1968 encyclical *Humanae Vitae* they won A Famous Victory. Not a victory in changing the Church's teaching, but a victory in persuading many, perhaps most, Catholics that they can ignore such teaching with spiritual impunity. In this they were greatly aided by supine prelates who learned to turn a blind eye to dissent and deviance more generally, one of the consequences of which is detailed in the files of your local prosecutor. After contraception, there was agitation for married priests, then for priestesses, then for the moral approval of homosexuality. And, all along, the demand for the "democratizing" of church government, sometimes called power sharing, which, being translated, means the quest for power. Sex, power, and license drove the discontinuant cause of the left, which no doubt still inspires some as, toddling about the nursing home garden, they reminisce about grand battles past.

It would be not only churlish but also inaccurate to deny that they loved the Church, or, at the very least, that they loved the Church that would have been more lovable if she had submitted to their reformist ministrations. Many of them spoke, and some still speak, of their love-hate relationship with the Church. They were persuaded that they acted in the service of the Church to make her more relevant and appealing to people like themselves, or to people whom they wanted to be like. They were not moved by the objection that, were all their demands to be met, the Catholic Church would be much like, say, the Episcopal Church. They are Catholic, they insisted, and being Catholic matters, even if they could not specify exactly how or why. To the observation that their Catholic Church would look like the Episcopal Church, they respond with touching naïveté that such a thing could not happen. After all, this is the Catholic Church, they say. Thus do they claim to have more confidence in the Catholic Church than their critics; they forget that the Episcopal Church and all the other churches were once part of the Catholic Church as well. We know that the Catholic Church, because she is the Catholic Church, will not go the way of all denominational flesh. That does not mean that she and many who belong to her cannot be severely damaged by those who would lead in that direction.

In more lucid moments, the discontinuants of the left know they have lost on the issues. The discipline of celibacy is precisely that, a discipline and not a doctrine. It conceivably could be made optional, but if it were I believe it would be exceptional and shadowed by the suspicion of sexual deviance. In the wake of the sex-abuse scandals, the determination of the Church's leadership, here and in Rome, is to strengthen, not weaken, the discipline of celibacy understood as perfect and perpetual chastity. On ordaining women, twenty centuries of tradition, reaffirmed by the Magisterium in a manner that the Congregation for the Doctrine of the Faith terms infallible, says that the Church is simply not authorized to do it. And, as noted earlier, even were there a doubt, the Church cannot ordain in doubt without jeopardizing the entire sacramental economy. In addition, it would be the end of all hope for reconciliation with Orthodoxy. Likewise, to declare that homosexual acts are rightly ordered according to law both natural and divine would be a reversal of millennia of unanimous teaching. It will not happen. One says that with the same confidence that one says two plus three will never equal six, or that the sun will rise tomorrow, or that the Catholic Church will continue to be the Catholic Church, or that the promise of Jesus that he will send the Spirit to lead and keep the Church in the truth can be trusted.

So the leftist party of discontinuity has lost on its chosen issues. There is still power sharing, however, and it is evident that over the centuries rules and patterns of government in the Church have varied. Bishops have been elected by popular acclaim. Remember the fourth century and Ambrose in Milan. But that was a long time ago. I see that in a recent column

Father Richard McBrien of Notre Dame writes, "Those who advocate for a more accountable and responsible pastoral leadership are not innovators. For various reasons, this element got lost in the ecclesiastical shuffle during the Second Christian Millennium when the Catholic Church became more deliberately monarchical in structure." Now there is the voice of a true traditionalist. You do remember "the ecclesiastical shuffle" of the second millennium, don't you? One is reminded of unreconstructed Southerners who speak of the Civil War as "the recent unpleasantness."

Of course bishops should be more accountable and responsible. That is, they should be better leaders, and the most important part of that is that they should lead with the zeal of the apostles whose successors they are. In the wake of the scandals, the enhanced awareness is that the bishops should be more, not less, the bishops that they are ordained to be. The problem was timorous shepherds who failed to protect the flock, and especially the lambs, fearing to confront the clerical wolves who had been admitted to the sheepfold. But power sharing understood as lay participation in decisionmaking is not an issue to sustain a cause or stir the soul. "Honey, remember tomorrow night you have the priorities-planning task force of the vicariat subcommittee on education finance." As Oscar Wilde said of socialism, the problem with ecclesiastical power sharing is that it leaves one with no free evenings.

How can it be that—with issues so doomed or dull and with a hoary-headed leadership that has to dredge up grievances from a distant past unknown to anyone born in the last fifty years—the discontinuants of the left can still present themselves as the vanguard of change? It's a good question. Here, speaking recently, is a bishop who belongs to the shrinking liberal caucus that was led by Archbishop Rembert Weakland of Milwaukee before he resigned in disgrace: "As priests in the Church we have a golden opportunity to become involved at the heart of this reawakening, of being forerunners of the Church of tomorrow, of being molders and builders of new theological language and ecclesial structures which speak to our contemporary society and which ensure a fresh hearing for the Christian message."

Bracing stuff, that. Some apparently still think so. Never mind that the bishop presides over a dispirited diocese of zero vocations, declining Mass attendance, closed schools, and an epidemic of scandals. Never mind that he hasn't read a serious book of theology for twenty years or that his assertions about the Christian message contain no reference to Christ. Never mind all that and much else; he is building "the Church of tomorrow." Having made a shambles of the Church of past and present, he has no choice but to bet on tomorrow. He is loyal to the Church, meaning the Church of tomorrow. He is obedient to the pope, meaning the next pope or maybe the one after that. So how, in the midst of the ruins of its own making, does the cause of leftist discontinuity maintain its status as the vanguard? In large part, simply by repeating, until reiteration overwhelms reflection, that it is the vanguard.

The delusion was also sustained because it was echoed through the general media. The media's dominant story line regarding the Church—sometimes, or so it seems, the only story line—is that of progressive dissidents challenging an authoritarian and ossified church leadership. It is always David vs. Goliath. Never mind that David is by now a septuagenarian.

The Church is ever so much older and bigger, and thus can forever be depicted as Goliath. When one gets weary and is afflicted by doubts about playing David, it no doubt helps to be assured by the *New York Times* that one is on the cutting edge of inevitable change. It is no little thing to be depicted as the champion of such great goods as intellectual inquiry and academic freedom. The anointed paladins of change have, it seems, little occasion or inclination to reflect on their unoriginality.

In 1959, Harold Rosenberg wrote on "The Tradition of the New," and he came up with the marvelous phrase "a herd of independent minds."[1] Frequently, the canonical list of complaints is pressed by invoking opinion polls allegedly showing that a majority of Catholics disagree with Church teaching on this or that. This is presented as an argument for change. Usually, it is evidence of unfaithful or ineffective preaching and catechesis. It is slight wonder that the faithful are confused—and, by now, more than a little bored—by priests who display their independence of mind by reiterating the daily newspaper's opinion of Catholic teaching.

At times the traditionalists of the new are amusingly counterfactual. During those memorable days in Rome surrounding the death of John Paul and the election of Benedict, the media coverage was generally respectful, even reverent. But again and again reporters expressed their puzzlement at the outpouring of devotion for a faith that everybody knows is unacceptably outdated and oppressive. One moment stands out. Three million (some say 4 million) people came from all over the world to say their farewells and thank yous to John Paul. By my estimate and that of others, at least 70 percent were people younger than thirty-five. Behind an American television reporter, one saw hundreds of thousands of young people praying and singing as the reporter concluded the segment: "But the great question remains," she said, "whether an ancient and in many ways hidebound Church is still capable of making itself relevant to a new generation." She did not turn around to see the answer to her great question.

Yet it must be acknowledged that the discontinuants of the left do have a devotion to the Church. Once a Catholic always a Catholic, it is said. But their devotion goes deeper than that. They are relentlessly ecclesiocentric. They have no life apart from the institution of the Church. This is especially true of priests and nuns who have been in rebellion for forty years or more, but it is also true of many lay people who might be called professional Catholics. Their entire life story is one of battling the bad old pre–Vatican II Church to make way for the post–Vatican II Church that was not to be. Whatever the shambles they left in their wake, they have, to their mind, kept the faith. A great irony is that the actual faith, as articulated by the Second Vatican Council, stressed the mission of the Church in the world and to the world. Totally absorbed by intra-Church quarrels, the traditionalists of the new have lived their lives in an ecclesiocentric box. Their incessant "calls to action" are to change the Church, not the world. It is not simply that such ecclesiocentric activism leaves one with no free evenings; it is a distraction from the worldly tasks to which the Council called the Catholic people.

Lay people in particular need, with the spirited encouragement of the clergy, to get on with their lives of being faithful Catholics in the family, in the workplace, in business, in the arts, in the sciences, and wherever God is calling them to be faithful. Those who do get on with their lives generally want to leave the government of the Church to the bishops and those whose job it is. They may at times be disappointed, even grievously disappointed, by the bishops, but they know that they have their responsibilities and the bishops have theirs. They may have difficulties with the teaching of the Church on questions such as women's ordination or homosexuality, but they know that teaching will not be changed, and they deeply intuit that teaching *should* not be changed by their agitation for change. Although they are willing to give counsel and help out as they can, they are not prepared to exchange their vocations in the world for a life of ecclesiastical activism.

Relentless futurism provides unlimited escapes from the counterevidence of the present. This works in all kinds of wondrous ways. Remember, for instance, how the Jesuits were once noted for their fierce loyalty to the papacy. They are still loyal, but they bring a futurist twist of discontinuant devising. Thus the influential Karl Rahner, in one of his less judicious moments, told his fellow Jesuits: "You must remain loyal to the papacy in theology and in practice, because that is part of your heritage to a special degree, but because the actual form of the papacy remains subject, in the future too, to an historical process of change, your theology and ecclesiastical law has above all to serve the papacy as it will be in the future." The Jesuit Paul Shaughnessy comments: "Jesuits are all loyal to the papacy, but to the future papacy—that of Pope Chelsea XII, perhaps—and their support for contraception, gay sex, and divorce proceeds from humble obedience to this conveniently protean pontiff."[2] Father Shaughnessy goes too far, of course. There are still some admirably loyal Jesuits. But sleight of hand is evident. As with the above-mentioned bishop, all things are permitted when one is a "forerunner of the Church of tomorrow." Being a faithful Catholic is becoming now what being Catholic will mean when faithfulness is redefined. Liberated by "the spirit of Vatican II" from past and present, discontinuants of the left hold themselves rigorously accountable to a future of their own desiring.

A *New Yorker* cartoon has executives sitting around the boardroom table on which is a box of soap emblazoned with the word "NEW!!!" The chairman is saying, "What do you mean what's new about it? The 'New!!!' on the box is what's new." For almost forty weary years, the left has managed to sell itself as the Church of the future by incessantly announcing that it is the Church of the future. And the pitch does sell, in part because it appears to be news. It is merely pseudo-news, but it is welcome news to those who dislike the Church of the past and the present. This is crucial to understanding the success of the leftist party of discontinuity. From the beginning, from John XXIII's announcement of a council, the story line was established that there must be something very wrong with the Church of the past and present or else the Pope would not have called a council to set things right. And much was wrong with the Church, as there always will be. But in the generally received story line of the Council, the depiction of problem and remedy was seriously skewed.

It is impossible to overestimate the influence of Xavier Rynne (also known as the late Fr. Francis X. Murphy) in establishing that story line. Almost all Catholics get their news about the Church from the general media, and almost all the media followed the story line set by Rynne in his voluminous reports in the *New Yorker*. The first piece of the story line to be put into place is that the Church is an institution like any other, and that its self-protective power structure is dominated by recalcitrant conservatives and challenged by courageous liberals. Theological language about the Church—as in "We believe in one, holy, catholic, and apostolic Church"—is, in this view, a smokescreen employed to hide the real questions, which are questions of privilege and power. To be sure, the Church is a thoroughly, but not exhaustively, human and social institution. But if she is not what she claims to be in language inescapably theological and sacramental, she is no more than another institutional "it" among many institutional "its," albeit a very big and old and venerable "it."

An element of sweet justice appeared in 2005, forty years after Xavier Rynne's reporting on the Council, when the same *New Yorker* published an insightful report by Peter J. Boyer, "A Hard Faith."[3] Boyer writes:

> *When it was revealed that the new Pope was Cardinal Joseph Ratzinger, who had adopted the name Benedict XVI, Father Richard McBrien, a Notre Dame University theologian interpreting the event for American television, was plainly taken aback. Asked his response, McBrien hesitated, and then said, "Surprised." The day before, McBrien had predicted that the College of Cardinals surely would not select Ratzinger as the next Pontiff, and warned that if Ratzinger became Pope "thousands upon thousands of Catholics in Europe and the United States would roll their eyes and retreat to the margins of the Church." Now McBrien urged patience. There was some chance that Benedict might rise to his new station; in any*

case, McBrien said, "he is seventy-eight. We're not talking about a long pontificate."

Boyer observes: "Progressives had lived in a suspended mood of *fin de regime* for a very long time, which was occasionally expressed as an impatience with the old man's [John Paul II's] stubborn postponement of the inevitable. Now he was dead, and still his regime lived." Peter Boyer traveled the country observing and talking with leaders of the renewal movements mentioned earlier, and with today's younger priests and seminarians. Everywhere he discovered a vibrant orthodoxy on the rise among those who identified themselves as "John Paul II Catholics," those who are now "Benedict Catholics," which is to say Catholics who are grateful to live with and under Peter among us.

Boyer spent time with the exceedingly personable Archbishop Charles Chaput of Denver who has sparked a "reform of the reform" on many fronts, including the building of a seminary that is attracting abundant candidates for the priesthood. Chaput has also been a lightning rod for the critics of Catholic assertiveness in the public square. "Whenever the Church is criticized," Chaput says, "she understands herself better and is purified. And when she is purified, she better serves the Lord. We're at a time in our country when some Catholics—too many—are discovering that they've gradually become non-Catholics who happen to go to Mass. That's sad and difficult, and a judgment on a generation of Catholic leadership. But it may be exactly the moment of truth the Church needs." His goal, of course, is not that such Catholics leave the Church but that they become *Catholics* who go to Mass.

Many of the most talented in that earlier generation of leadership said they wanted to "demystify" the Church. They ended up by abandoning the mystery. This de-theologizing and de-sacramentalizing of our understanding of the Church is now widespread. Consider a small but telling incident. An archbishop in the Northeast is addressing lay leaders on the years of scandal and wants to end on an upbeat note. With a warm and winning smile, he declares, "I'm here to tell you we got a great church!" This is a bishop of the one, holy, catholic, and apostolic Church. Imagine, if you can, Ambrose or Aquinas or John Paul II saying, "We got a great church." I know, you can't. Neither can I. What kind of operative ecclesiology is in the archbishop's mind and heart? Maybe "The Catholic Church, Inc." Or the voluntary association with the biggest and best niche in the religious marketplace. Like a basketball coach during a losing streak: "I'm here to tell you we got a great team!" Yes, it's a little incident, but implicit in it are the ravages wreaked by the construal of Vatican II in discontinuity from the story of the mystical Body of Christ through time.

It may be objected that, although I started out by saying there is a party of continuity (the Catholic center) and a party of discontinuity, the latter having left and right branches, I have been speaking mainly about the left branch of the party of discontinuity. There is a good reason for that. From the very first session of the Council, beginning October 11, 1962, the perception of the Council was controlled by Rynne and like-minded reporters, and they soon imposed upon it the master template that there were only two parties in play—the liberals and the conservatives. The right-wing discontinuants were simply "conservative extremists" who were beyond the pale and unworthy of notice, except when it was convenient to depict all conservatives as extremists. This was a masterful move, and it continues to be—in the general media and much of the Catholic media—the dominant story line in explaining the Second Vatican Council. Leftist discontinuants constituted the force of "progress" that prevailed against the party of continuity and against rightists deploring discontinuity, both of the latter being portrayed as the party of conservative resistance.

By the second session, everybody "knew" that the Council was about an archconservative Catholic Church set against the modern world and belatedly being dragged into the twentieth century. Indeed—wonder of wonders—Catholicism was becoming the champion of liberalism's tale of historical progress. Popularizing theologians who fit this master template were made the experts on the Council. Those who disagreed were routinely dismissed as the conservative resistance. A priest friend recalls going to a press conference at the Gregorian University, where the great Father John Courtney Murray, who had a major influence on the Council's teaching on religious freedom, was trying to explain to the media the complexities of what had happened at the Council that day. He was followed by Father Charles Davis, then a leftist popularizer who later left the priesthood and the Church when he recognized that he was no longer a Catholic. Father Davis began, "Well, it's really quite simple. The conservatives . . ." My friend looked over at Fr. Murray, who was sadly shaking his head in disagreement. But the progressive vs. conservative story line was by then firmly established.

And so it has been until recently. The great leaders of the theological, liturgical, ecumenical, and pastoral movements of renewal affirmed by the Council are, I expect, still—if sadness is permitted in heaven—sadly shaking their heads in disagreement. One hears them saying, "That is not what the Council said. That is not what it said at all." While those leaders were still with us, Hans Küng, later officially decertified as a Catholic theologian, rejected Karl Rahner's criticism of his ecclesiology as being essentially Protestant. Leslie Dewart, later associated with "death of God" theology, rejected Bernard Lonergan's criticism of his work as a false de-hellenization of doctrine. The Jesuit provincials rejected the pleas of Murray and Lonergan, their most eminent theologians, to maintain the tradition of serious intellectual formation. In the name of "the spirit of the Council," liberal French theologians, following the revolutionary ritual of turning against the fathers, dismissed as impossibly outdated the giants who had prepared the way for the Council: Jean Daniélou, Yves Congar, Henri de Lubac, Louis Bouyer, and Jacques Maritain. It was a clean sweep for the discontinuants of the left.

Bishops and religious superiors turned to the popularizers to implement the Council, and the mostly sorry results are still with us today in theology, liturgy, catechesis, and much else. As mentioned earlier, *Humanae Vitae*'s attempted exercise of papal teaching authority in 1968 was handily turned back. The media portrayed *Humanae Vitae* as an effort to break the master template, to return to the bad old days of what was by then called "the pre–Vatican II Church." Paul VI reigned another ten years, but he never issued another encyclical. Even today, after twenty-six years of the pontificate of John Paul II, who was preeminently "a man of the Council," the template has not disappeared. But it began to crack long ago, and now it is broken.

It was at a conference in the mid-1980s that I listened to Hans Küng hold forth in triumphalist tones on the victory of the progressives. "We" control, he announced, the seminaries, the academic departments of theology, the catechetical and liturgical institutions, the publishing houses, the magazines that matter, and the diocesan chanceries. Most of the bishops, he said, are now on "our" side, and those who aren't have been neutralized. Anyone who wants a future in the hierarchy or the Catholic academy has no choice but to cooperate, he observed. It was a clean sweep; all that was left were a few details; the disgruntled band of risibly reactionary dissidents from the new order didn't understand what had happened, and they couldn't do much about it.

It was a memorable speech, and the circumstance he described is today mainly a memory. Almost nobody on the left is talking that way today. They are still largely in control of some institutions, notably in the academy and some religious orders, but the more astute among them know that they are increasingly on the defensive. Their most reliable allies today, as in 1962, are people in the media who continue to see the Catholic Church as a reactionary and threatening institution, the great and not-to-be-tolerated dissenter from the gospel of liberal progress. For such people, the only good Catholic is a bad Catholic. Those in the anti-Catholic sector of our "high culture"—and it is large and of considerable influence—need the discontinuant left, and it needs them. Without this alliance of mutual need, the master template is itself but a memory.

It is no secret that the initiative today is with the center. For younger clergy and seminarians, the so-called bad old days are the olden days that their grandparents talked about. They were inspired by John Paul II, the only pope they had ever known; and, before Cardinal Ratzinger became Pope Benedict XVI, many of them belonged to what was popularly called "the Ratzinger fan club." Renewal movements feed into and draw from the millions of young people gathered by, for instance, the World Youth Days. In American parishes, chancel dancers in leotards and clown Masses are—except for the backwaters of the vanguard that was—a thing of the past. Perhaps a few parishioners are still amused by Father Mike's clever homiletical sallies against Rome and the "institutional" church (as though there were any other kind). But the silly season is almost over, although elements of the discontinuant right find it useful to generate outrage by pretending that it is still in full swing.

True, what passes for theology in many nominally Catholic colleges is a tiresome deconstruction of orthodoxy, but that, I expect, leads many students to want to explore an orthodoxy that they never learned and that their teachers deem worthy of such intense attack. In Washington, D.C., in New York, in Boston, and elsewhere, there are growing and vibrant networks of young professionals excited about being Catholic. Many are discerning a vocation to the priesthood or the religious life. In the marvelous phrase of Archbishop Edwin O'Brien, young people will give their lives for a mystery but not for a question mark. By way of sharpest contrast, the discontinuant left is dying because there is no successor generation. It cannot replicate the bad old days, which alone gives meaning to its existence. A friend who has an inflated sense of irony says that the young orthodox of today will, in due course, impose a new and oppressive regime that will, in turn, give rise to another generation of rebellion. Although stranger things have happened, I do not think so. That hope, too, is a projection of the *fin de regime* mood described by Peter Boyer.

Consider the arguments to which some are now reduced. In *Commonweal* and the London *Tablet*, reviewers of George Weigel's bracing book of 2002, *The Courage to Be Catholic*, contend that "the center" is somewhere between Weigel and Garry Wills. Among discontinuant leftists, Wills is a radical. He's not waiting for Vatican III or the pope after the next pope. His position is that Vatican II dismantled once and for all the Magisterium and, with it, the teaching authority of the Church.[4] To save him embarrassment, I will call the *Commonweal* reviewer Mr. B. He has a carefully cultivated reputation as a "moderate" liberal. Mr. B says that his position is "the broad middle" between Weigel and Wills. What can this possibly mean?

Weigel stands solidly with millennia of tradition as set forth by the Council and authoritatively interpreted by three subsequent pontificates. Wills says that that tradition is a "structure of deceit," and John Paul was an authoritarian throwback who attempted "a coup against the Council." Where does that leave Mr. B and his broad middle? The successor of Peter, who according to Wills is certainly not the successor of Peter, is using a liberal council for reactionary purposes, but, despite the deceit, he had a winning personality and was, although certainly not John Paul the Great, maybe John Paul the Not All Bad. Weigel, to cite another example, greatly admires John Paul's "theology of the body." Wills says that magisterial teaching on sexuality is "just silly," and he touts contraception, gay rights, and a woman's right to choose. I will leave it to Mr. B to explain how he locates the "broad middle" between Weigel and Wills on these and other questions.

It is said that a liberal is someone who refuses to take his own side in an argument. Mr. B does not even have a side, or, if he does, it is an imagined space between clashing contradictions. To such implausibility does the master template of liberal vs. conservative reduce differences of momentous consequence. Mr. B. and many others are moderate members of the leftist party of discontinuity, of which Garry Wills is a radical member. They have in common that, for them, the center (i.e., the Magisterium) is the right. They are not on speaking terms with, and they hardly deign to recognize the existence of, their ideological cousins in the rightist branch of the party of discontinuity, for whom the center (i.e., the Magisterium) is the left. Yet they are one in agreeing that a choice must be made between the pre–Vatican II Church and the post–Vatican II Church, differing only in the choices they have made. Both insist that the Council was a radical break with the tradition, the difference being that the right deplores the putative break and the left celebrates it.

The party of continuity is the center. From the Council of Jerusalem to Vatican II, from Peter on through John Paul the Great and Benedict XVI, there is—variations, deviations, and ambiguities of history notwithstanding—a continuing and identifiable community that is the Catholic Church. There have over the centuries been much more powerful parties of discontinuity than we have experienced these past forty years. But the Catholic Church remains the continuing community to which Jesus promised he would send the Spirit, and the Spirit will lead us into, and keep us in, the truth. Even if one does not believe that promise, can anyone really believe that the likes of Garry Wills, on the left, or the Society of St. Pius

X, on the right, are the future of the Catholic Church? The extreme discontinuants of the left are angry because their understanding of Vatican II's promise of their preferred future has been broken. The extreme discontinuants of the right are angry because they believe Vatican II broke the Church's promise to maintain a preferred past. Both promises are the product of imaginations in different orbits. Both parties live off their anger; both live off the Church that they condemn. As for the Laodicean moderates such as Mr. B, they will, in their broadly middle way, continue to grumble incoherently about this and that. But I expect they are secretly grateful for the people who—inspired by the Second Vatican Council and in continuing communion with Peter—see visions and dream dreams for the renewal of the one Church that was, is, and will be until Our Lord returns in glory. Parties of discontinuity we will have with us always, but the center holds.

To say the center holds could be misleading. "Holds" may suggest a certain stasis, an immovable stability, and thus miss the drama of the matter. The aforementioned *New Yorker* article by Peter Boyer, as well as other commentaries on "the return of orthodoxy," might lead one to think that things are settling back into their routine, that the years of excitement are over, that the swinging pendulum has at last returned to the center. When the pendulum stops swinging, the clock has stopped, and that is certainly not what I mean in saying that the center holds. Orthodoxy is not stasis but the high adventure of fidelity to truth. This is the understanding caught by the inimitable G. K. Chesterton in his 1908 book *Orthodoxy*. Permit me a longish quotation that no one could wish to be shorter:

Last and most important, it is exactly this which explains what is so inexplicable to all the modern critics of the history of Christianity. I mean the monstrous wars about small points of theology, the earthquakes of emotion about a gesture or a word. It was only a matter of an inch; but an inch is everything when you are balancing. The Church could not afford to swerve a hair's breadth on some things if she was to continue her great and daring experiment of the irregular equilibrium. Once let one idea become less powerful and some other idea would become too powerful. It was no flock of sheep the Christian shepherd was leading, but a herd of bulls and tigers, of terrible ideals and devouring doctrines, each one of them strong enough to turn to a false religion and lay waste the world. Remember that the Church went in specifically for dangerous ideas; she was a lion tamer.

The idea of birth through a Holy Spirit, of the death of a divine being, of the forgiveness of sins, or the fulfillment of prophecies, are ideas which, any one can see, need but a touch to turn them into something blasphemous or ferocious. The smallest link was let drop by the artificers of the Mediterranean, and the lion of ancestral pessimism burst his chain in the forgotten forests of the north. Of these theological equalizations I have to speak afterwards.

Here it is enough to notice that if some small mistake were made in doctrine, huge blunders might be made in human happiness. A sentence phrased wrong about the nature of symbolism would have broken all the best statues in Europe. A slip in the definitions might stop all the dances; might wither all the Christmas trees or break all the Easter eggs. Doctrines had to be defined within strict limits, even in order that man might enjoy general human liberties The Church had to be careful, if only that the world might be careless.

This is the thrilling romance of Orthodoxy. People have fallen into a foolish habit of speaking of orthodoxy as something heavy, humdrum, and safe. There never was anything so perilous or so exciting as orthodoxy. It was sanity, and to be sane is more dramatic than to be mad. It was the equilibrium of a man behind madly rushing horses, seeming to stoop this way and to sway that, yet in every attitude having the grace of statuary and the accuracy of arithmetic. The Church in its early days went fierce and fast with any war-horse; yet it is utterly unhistoric to say that she merely went mad along one idea, like a vulgar fanaticism. She swerved to left and right, so exactly as to avoid enormous obstacles. She left on one hand the huge bulk of Arianism, buttressed by all the worldly powers to make Christianity too worldly. The next instant she was swerving to avoid an orientalism, which would have made it too unworldly.

The orthodox Church never took the tame course or accepted the conventions; the orthodox Church was never respectable. It would have been easier to have accepted the earthly power of the Arians. It would have been easy, in the Calvinistic seventeenth century, to fall into the bottomless pit of predestination. It is easy to be a madman; it is easy to be a heretic. It is always easy to let the age have its head; the difficult thing is to keep one's own. It is always easy to be a modernist; as it is easy to be a snob.

To have fallen into any of those open traps of error and exaggeration which fashion after fashion and sect after sect set along the historic path of Christendom—that would indeed have been simple. It is always simple to fall; there are an infinity of angles at which one falls, only one at which one stands. To have fallen into any one of the fads from Gnosticism to Christian Science would indeed have been obvious and tame. But to have avoided them all has been one whirling adventure; and in my vision the heavenly chariot flies thundering through the ages, the dull heresies sprawling and prostrate, the wild truth reeling but erect.

All of which is to say that the center holds or, as Chesterton puts it, the center stands, reeling but erect. And so I return to where we began, to the "Rome Diary" of those days of April 2005, days of solemn conclusion and new beginning in a story that is ever ancient, ever new.

8 | Rome Diary

Monday morning, April 11. Three days after the Requiem Mass for John Paul the Great, and I walked over to St. Peter's Square, where thousands upon thousands are lined up to see the place where they had put the body. Many were disappointed in their hope of seeing the body when, in the early hours of Friday morning, the basilica had to be closed for the Friday funeral. The crypt, I am told, will not be open to the public until tomorrow. There he lies in the place previously occupied by John XXIII, who has been moved up into the main church.

Of the 264 popes, 148 are buried in St. Peter's. In his last will and testament, revealed last week, John Paul indicated that he would like to be buried in Poland, but he said the wishes of the cardinals should be followed. They decided on St. Peter's. There was a rumor that Poles were asking that at least his heart should be buried in Poland, a very Polish thing to do. But he is intact in St. Peter's, the 149th.

These have been days that tax superlatives; their events beggar words. It is reported that from 4 to 5 million have journeyed to Rome to say goodbye, more than twice the population of the city. Yet everything has gone so smoothly. It seems that the city is more peaceful than usual. Huge crowds of mourners packed the square and the Via della Conciliazione, and stretched across the Tiber and into the side streets. People waited as long as twenty-six hours to enter the basilica, and then, on Friday, to get near the funeral. One hesitates to say that anything is historically unprecedented, but it seems certain that never in human history have so many from so many places in the world gathered to pay their final respects. He went to the world, and the world came to him. The Poles are especially prominent, waving their flag and singing hymns and national songs. After a thousand years of existence denied and despised by powerful neighbors, John Paul restored their nation, his nation, to a place of honor in the world.

At the funeral, more than a hundred nations were represented. With all the presidents, monarchs, prime ministers, and other dignitaries, security was not conspicuous, which probably means that it was very competent. Anyone familiar with the complex history of Catholicism and the American experiment could not help being struck by the presence of an American president, along with two former presidents, at the funeral of a pope. In the media and in conversations, however, nobody has remarked on this remarkable turn of events—but, then, his pontificate always turned the unprecedented into the taken-for-granted. It was unthinkable that President Bush would not be here. What was remarked was the large Jewish delegation and, even more remarked, the many representatives from Islamic nations. Among the titles of the pope is Pontifex Maximus, the great builder of bridges.

The funeral was exactly as it should have been. Solemn, pulling all the stops of sacred pomp, joining grief and gratitude in a grace-filled exultation of resurrection hope. Exactly right, too, was the homily by Joseph Cardinal Ratzinger, dean of the College of Cardinals. He made room for the frequent outbursts of sustained applause and shouts of the crowd that John Paul be declared a saint, and be declared so right now.

There was a time in the ancient Church, long before procedures for canonization were codified in the sixteenth century, when saints were declared by popular acclamation, and it almost looked yesterday as though that might happen again. And the shout went up, "Magnus! Magnus!"

For many years I had written that he would be called John Paul the Great, and I do believe it is happening. Of the millions who came to say goodbye, the clear majority were young people in their teens or twenties. Among those impressed by this astonishing response are the cardinals who will elect the next pope, and some of them are saying today that the better part of wisdom is to stay the course of John Paul's pontificate. If continuity is what they are looking for, that may speak well for Cardinal Ratzinger, who is so closely identified with the major initiatives of John Paul. Even before yesterday, he was on everybody's list of leading *papabili*.

It takes determination not to discern a providential hand in the convergence of events from the beginning of Holy Week through the funeral of the pope. All in all, the major media made an effort to rise to the occasion. There were notable exceptions: On the *Lehrer News Hour,* I was pitted the other day against the egregious Alan Wolfe, of Boston College, who railed against Republicans for politicizing the death of Terri Schiavo, thereby politicizing the judiciously countenanced crime in a manner most base. All the great champions of "choice" were determined that a brain-damaged woman in a Florida nursing facility, a woman who had no choice and was sustained by nothing but food and water, be made dead. A few days later, the death of John Paul commanded the front page; but a large special section of recycled conventional wisdom about Terri Schiavo appeared in the *New York Times,* along with an editorial drawing the moral that the pope's rigid teaching about the sanctity of life had denied Terri Schiavo the death with dignity that John Paul himself enjoyed. When will they ever learn?

But, for the most part, the media coverage of the pope's death has been intelligent, respectful, and even reverential. Although there is no way to measure the effect, this has been an extraordinary moment of evangelization. There was the small distraction of the death of Prince Rainier of Monaco, and the much larger distraction of the tawdry "royal wedding" of Prince Charles to his mistress of many years, a wedding postponed for one day so that Charles could attend the papal funeral.

I am here in Rome to co-host with Raymond Arroyo the daily broadcasts of EWTN, the international television network founded by the formidable Mother Angelica, whose biography Raymond has just completed. He tells a truly remarkable story, one filled with mystery, miracles, brains, and guts. My agreement with EWTN is not exclusive, so I am working also with other print and broadcast media.

George Weigel, the author of the definitive biography of John Paul, *Witness to Hope,* is here under exclusive contract with NBC and is largely responsible for that network's generally excellent coverage. Rome in my experience is endless conversations over lunch and dinner, mainly with media types and with friends and acquaintances in the worlds within worlds of the universal Church variously connected to the nerve center that is the Holy See. The plan is to stay here through the conclave, which begins April 18 and is expected to produce a new pope within two to four days. EWTN is broadcasting from a jerry-built booth that, from its perch atop the North American College, enjoys a magnificent view overlooking St. Peter's. (The North American College—or, as it is called, the NAC—is often described as the West Point of the Church in the United States, a place where bishops send promising seminarians.) Other television networks had to be satisfied with the roof of the Urbaniana, an institute for mission churches, next door.

Most of the talk is about the next pope, with regular references to "the legacy of John Paul II." It seems that almost every interview begins with the question "What do you think is the chief legacy of John Paul II?" I have by now refined in response a dozen riffs on his "prophetic humanism," his proposing and not imposing a more promising future for the human project, and related themes. There are only so many things one can say in three or four minutes, and one easily wearies of saying them.

Many years ago, when I was a young Lutheran pastor, I complained to my older friend Rabbi Abraham Joshua Heschel about the tedium of the lecture circuit. "The worst thing," I said, "is that you get tired of hearing yourself saying the same things. Last week I was in Kansas City talking about Christianity and racial justice, and this Saturday I will be in Chicago talking about Christianity and racial justice." Heschel listened patiently as I went on in this vein and then said, "Nuh, Richard, so you think in Chicago they know what you said in Kansas City? Go to Chicago, Richard. Go to Chicago." When on airplanes going I know not where or why, I have over the years often heard the voice of Heschel, "Go to Chicago, Richard. Go to Chicago." And so I once again manage to perk up and respond to the questions "What is the chief legacy of John Paul II" and "Who will be the next pope?"

In Rome and in circles closely connected to Rome, the chatter about the next pope begins the day a new pope is installed. It was understandably more intense during the last several years of John Paul's undeniable decline. Most of the talk is idle speculation, as idle as it is inevitable. For the record, this is the state of the chatter shortly after the funeral of John Paul:

First in alphabetical order and the sentimental favorite of many is Cardinal Arinze of Nigeria. With long years of experience in the Curia, Arinze has many friends in the United States. Our magazine, *First Things,* hosted him in New York last year for an ecumenical theological conference. As usual, he was disarmingly charming and candid in response to even the most difficult questions. Many of us think it would be a great thing to have a black African pope, but we don't have a vote. The consensus is that Arinze, although greatly admired, has slight chance of election. "The Church is not ready for an African pope," it is said. That can be read in many ways, some less edifying than others.

Jorge Mario Bergoglio of Buenos Aires is high on every list. Known as an incisive thinker and intensely holy man living an austere life, it is held against him that he is a Jesuit, although he has suffered the slings and arrows of fellow Jesuits of a more "progressive" bent. No member of a religious order has been elected pope since 1831.

If the Italians recapture the office, their man could be Tarcisio Bertone of Genoa, a close associate of Ratzinger.

Dario Castrillion Hoyos of Colombia, Claudio Hummes of Sao Paulo, and Oscar Rodriguez Maradiago of Honduras are Latin Americans mentioned. The last is young and eager, some think too young and too eager.

Ivan Dias of Bombay is an astute theologian who has shown the way in protecting Catholic integrity in the engagement with religious pluralism.

Among other Italians is Giovanni Battista Re, long in curial experience but lacking a pastoral track record.

Camillo Ruini, vicar of Rome, is highly respected and was very close to John Paul.

Dionigi Tettamanzi of Milan is something of a populist in his appeal and an expert in bioethics, a field of growing interest in moral theology. A cardinal from Scotland refers to him as "the wee fat fellow."

My impression is that Angelo Scola of Venice may be the leading Italian candidate, but that is perhaps because I have been listening to my friends, who are also his friends; they are greatly impressed by his intellectual and pastoral skills, which are combined with a deep spirituality.

Christoph Schoenborn of Vienna is often mentioned, but it is deemed a liability that he is young (for a pope) and, or so it is said, he has shown very limited progress in revitalizing the Church in Austria.

The only plausible English-speaking *papabile* is the formidable George Pell of Sydney, Australia. He is a friend and I confess that I would rejoice in his election, but that seems an unlikely prospect. (The same is true of Francis George of Chicago, but it is thought to be a certainty that no American could be elected, and I tend to agree with the reasons for that.)

It would, I think, be a very good thing to have a pope from Africa, Latin America, or Asia, but the odds favor an Italian. The real alternative is Ratzinger. His election would spark a firestorm of negative reaction from "progressives" in Western Europe and the United States. There is little love for Germans, and his long and thankless work as the chief doctrinal officer under John Paul has earned him a reputation as the "enforcer" of orthodoxy. Ratzinger is, in fact, a man of great personal charm and profound holiness. In 1988, I invited him to give our annual Erasmus Lecture. The lecture, held in midtown Manhattan, was disrupted by a hundred or more gay activists who shouted pleasantries such as "Sieg Heil!"; "Nazi Ratzy!"; and "Inquisitor Go Home!" I finally called in the police to restore order. Before resuming his lecture, Ratzinger offered a spontaneous reflection on the integrity of intellectual discourse and the impossibility of civilization without civility. Those, he said, were truths that were impressed upon him during the Hitler era, and the not entirely dissimilar student revolution of 1968.

Throughout the raucous events at the Erasmus Lecture, Ratzinger was the very picture of tranquillity. He spoke not one harsh word. In the ecumenical conference held during the days following the public lecture, he won the respect and affection of the participating theologians. I thought of those days while listening to his homily at John Paul's funeral in which he winsomely displayed a pastoral dimension that many had not suspected. Although Joseph Ratzinger is guaranteed to be labeled "controversial," his election would, I believe, be reassuring to many and would provide the Church with leadership in secure continuity with John Paul the Great. Not that it will affect the outcome, but he is my candidate, and I persist in thinking he will be elected.

But again, this is all speculation. The new pope will be chosen during the next days or weeks, and faithful Catholics will have no doubt that he is the choice of the Holy Spirit. He may be chosen to advance the great springtime of renewal of which John Paul so often spoke, or he may be chosen to test our faith. Either way, he will be the 265th successor of Peter, and we will, with full assent of heart and mind, acknowledge him as the shepherd of Christ's pilgrim Church on earth, as Peter among us.

But now, in the immediate aftermath of the funeral, we are keenly aware that, whoever he is, he will not be, nobody could be, another John Paul II. That would be too much to expect. As we had no right to expect the inestimable gift of the man to whom and for whom we now, in grief and gratitude, offer our thanks.

Wednesday, April 13. This is the week of the great pause before the conclave begins next Monday. A pause must be filled, and people are not particular about the quality of the filling. Yesterday, the distraction was Bernard Cardinal Law presiding in St. Peter's at the Mass of the second day of mourning. Yes, the protocol is that the pastors (arch-priests, as they are called) of the Roman basilicas preside at these first Masses, and he is pastor of St. Mary Major; but he could have declined the honor, and should have. In full awareness of all that he did and did not do in Boston, I have considerable respect for Cardinal Law, but nobody needed during these solemn days the reopening of wounds from the sex-abuse scandal in the United States. Although SNAP, the "survivor network," managed to get only one demonstrator here to protest Law's prominent appearance, the media made the most of it.

In truth, Law has paid a price for his negligence in Boston, being demoted from the archbishop of a major see to the pastor of a church in Rome, albeit a distinguished church. But he continues to serve on seven major congregations here, including those dealing with clergy and the appointment of bishops. And that galls many in the United States, who think he should be on bread and water in a remote hermitage. That sentiment may be vindictive, but it is also true that many here in Rome seem not to appreciate the intensity of disgust and outrage with the scandals in the United States. The brouhaha over his presiding at the Mass will likely not last through the next news cycle, but it was a sour note that easily could have been avoided.

Some cardinals have declared themselves "shaken" or "shaken up" by the enthusiasm of the youthful crowds at the funeral last Friday. After twenty-six-plus years, they show surprise at the powerful response of young people to John Paul II. That they say they were surprised strikes me as surprising. The millions who poured into Rome to say goodbye were not all young, but they were united in the repeated shouts of "Santo subito! Santo subito!"—make him a saint and do it now. Many prelates are taking up the cry, and there is reportedly a petition being circulated advocating that the usual steps toward beatification and canonization be bypassed. The usual thing is to wait five years after a candidate's death before his cause is even entered, but an exception was made for Mother Teresa, and some think a bigger exception should be made for John Paul. Already miracles attributed to John Paul II are being reported, but the miracles that count in this connection are the ones that occur after the person's death.

Saint-making or, more precisely, the official recognition of saints, was a big interest of the late pope. Since the procedures were codified in the late sixteenth century, 784 saints have been canonized, more than half of them, 482, by John Paul. Of the 1,338 he beatified, 1,032 were martyrs; and of the 482 canonized, 402 were martyrs. He never tired of reminding us of the significance of the martyrs, and that the past hundred years has been the century of martyrs. No matter how his cause is handled, it is obvious that the popular acclamation of "Santo Subito!" and "Ioannes Paulus Magnus!" has had an impact here.

There is also much discussion today of a corrected translation of his last will and testament that suggests he really wanted to be buried in Poland. Apparently, that is not to be, although it is possible that the body could be taken from the former tomb of John XXIII, where it now lies, and transported to Poland. That seems unlikely because it would accent the ethnic nature of the pontificate and play into the hands of those who were given to referring derisively to "this Polish Pope." Another item filling the news vacuum is a report that John Paul told friends this past year that the three cardinals who could best carry on his mission are Ivan Dias of Bombay, Claudio Hummes of Sao Paulo, and Angelo Scola of Venice. I am told the report is being taken seriously by some cardinals, and not only by the three supposedly mentioned. The source of the report is unknown, and the whole thing strikes me as improbable in the extreme.

The permanent and mainly Italian reporters covering the Vatican—those called *vaticanisti*—are productive of rumors printed as fact. They have largely freed themselves from quaint journalistic inhibitions about documenting sources and related niceties. American and European reporters, on the other hand, are more inclined to indulge fantasies of cardinalatial campaigning and ambitions along the lines of secular politics.

My own impression is different. Few cardinals want to be pope or think they could be elected pope. They are earnestly looking for someone who can secure and advance the achievements of the pontificate past through combining the continuity of teaching with an effective outreach to the world, and especially to the young. They also know that the one whom they elect will likely be their leader for the rest of their own ministries. The great question, as one influential cardinal tells me, is this: "To whom can we confidently entrust the leadership of the Church?" On this seventh day of official mourning, four days away from the start of the conclave, that way of putting the matter would appear to point toward Joseph Cardinal Ratzinger.

There is the old saying that a cardinal going into the conclave as pope will certainly come out a cardinal. Of course that is not always true. In the modern era, a conclave has in several instances elected the person widely expected to be elected. Pius XII and Paul VI are cases in point. Today, the focus on Ratzinger is such that one informed observer asks me whether I think his nonelection would be construed as a rejection of the man and his work. Definitely not, or so it seems to me. We are still at an early point in the process and there are many possibilities to be explored. Last night on the broadcast I read a poem that John Paul II composed several years ago. In the poem he is anticipating this conclave:

> *The colors of the Sistine will then speak the word*
> *of the Lord:*
> *Tu es Petrus—once heard by Simon, son of John.*

Then John Paul II looks back to his own election:

> *So it was in August, and again in October,*
> *in the memorable year of the two conclaves,*

and so it will be once more, when the time comes,
after my death.
Do not forget: Omnia nuda et aperta sunt ante
  oculos Eius.
You who see all, point to him!
He will point him out . . .

I expect that is the truth of which electors are now keenly aware: "In the eyes of God all stand naked"—awaiting, in the words of John Paul, the action obedient to the "final transparency and light; the clarity of events, the clarity of conscience."

Thursday, April 14. Returning from a meeting over by the Borgo about noon, I am accosted by two well-dressed young men in front of the Congregation of the Doctrine of the Faith, just off St. Peter's Square. They are handing out flyers with a photo of their candidate and the legend "Santo Subito. Godfried. Your New Pope." The reference is to Godfried Cardinal Daneels of Belgium, and the two young Belgians, taking me to be an American cardinal, tell me that I should vote for Daneels because he is "pro-women and pro-condom." These Europeans are so sophisticated. *Santo Subito*—"Make him a saint and do it now"—is, of course, the popular cry for the more or less immediate canonization of John Paul II, a cry endorsed, I am told today, by a majority of the cardinals here. Doing that would require a suspension of the rules, but not nearly so dramatic a suspension as canonizing Daneels who is, to all appearances, far from being dead.

One may be sure that Daneels is not behind the antics of his enthusiastic supporters, and no informed source thinks he has even a remote chance of being elected next week. A noteworthy fact is that the party that styles itself "progressive" has no serious candidate in this process. They viewed Paul VI and, especially, John Paul II as aberrations to be endured until the election of "the next pope" who would agree with them and therefore be deserving of their obedience. For years, their dream candidate was Carlo Maria Martini, a Jesuit who has retired as Archbishop of Milan. In the absence of a plausible candidate, a few diehards are reduced to handing out campaign flyers for Godfried Daneels. The unusual thing is that these progressive activists were young, while most of the progressive party are tired and long in tooth. They still talk about the revolution they believe was mandated by "the spirit of Vatican II," but one senses that their hearts are not in it.

I ran into Fr. Andrew Greeley at Armando's last night. He is setting aside his next bodice-ripping novel in favor of writing a book about this conclave. John Allen, the immeasurably more responsible reporter on matters Roman, says he is also writing what he does not hesitate to describe as a "quickie" book on the conclave. Come September, it seems there will be at least half a dozen such books on the market. In his *Chicago Sun-Times* column this morning, Greeley complains that the Vatican has "raised secrecy to the status of a religion." He is unhappy with Cardinal Ratzinger's suggestion to the cardinals, in their first formal meeting after the funeral, that they decline all interviews with the media. As it happens, some cardinals were also unhappy with the suggestion, and it was finally agreed that they limit interviews to discussing John Paul II and the achievements of his pontificate. It appears that almost all cardinals are observing the agreement.

Among reporters and, more important, among informed members of the Curia there is considerable speculation in favor of Ratzinger. Others say that, although he will go into the conclave with most votes, the cardinals will certainly turn to someone less "controversial." Next Monday, as dean of the college of cardinals, he will preside at the Mass for the election of a pope (*Pro Eligendo Pontifice*) and, following up on his very well-received homily at the funeral, will have another opportunity to frame the questions to be addressed in the conclave.

If, for whatever reason, Ratzinger is not elected or declines election, the great question is who, if anyone, he will name as his preference. Here the speculation turns chiefly to Camillo Ruini, John Paul's vicar for Rome. Another possibility prominently mentioned is Ivan Dias, archbishop of Bombay, whose robust campaign for orthodoxy in the face of an Asian drift toward syncretism has earned him great respect. But, of course, other names I have mentioned in earlier diary entries are still in play. The rumor du jour, however, is that the Latin Americans are not agreed on a candidate and have decided that their turn will come with the next conclave, which may be ten or twenty years off.

Apart from the obvious desire of the Italians to resume what they view as their rightful control of the papacy, geographical factors seem to be playing no great role in this process—contrary to earlier expectations. Cardinal George of Chicago mentioned the other day that one criterion for a new pope is that "he is acceptable to the Italians." It is easy to forget that for centuries the papacy was an Italian monopoly. The cardinals were all Roman, and even today they are still nominally so (in that each cardinal has a titular church in the diocese of Rome). The College of Cardinals began to be significantly internationalized under Pius XII, and today Italians make up less than 20 percent of the electors. To say a pope must be acceptable to the Italians means, at the very least, that he speaks a passable Italian. Karol Wojtyla won their hearts when, in his first words upon being presented on the loggio of St. Peter's, he asked the Italians to correct him if he made mistakes in speaking "our"—at first he said "your"—language.

The daily broadcasts with EWTN provide a magnificent catechetical opportunity. With a mainly American audience in mind, we had Mary Ann Glendon of Harvard Law School on one evening; she addressed women in the Church, the mission of the laity, and her unique experiences in representing the Holy See in international conferences. Last night it was Michael Novak on the 1991 encyclical, *Centesimus Annus,* dealing with the free and just society; and this evening we will have seminarians from the North American College on how they discerned their vocation to the priesthood. In addition, there will be the legendary Fr. Peter Gumpel. Very old and very alert, Fr. Gumpel is with the dicastery that deals with the causes of saints, and I expect he will have some cautionary words about the popular cry (*Santo Subito!*) for expediting the canonization of John Paul II. He has also been a staunch defender of Pius XII against the many calumnies hurled at that good and brave man, and I definitely want to ask him about that.

Speaking of possible candidates for the papacy, one influential American remarked, "It is a comfort that we have such a strong bench." The others at the dinner table, myself included, looked at him with incredulity. The serious *papabili* would seem to be no more than four or five, all of whom I have mentioned in these notes. Of course, the Holy Spirit, as is the way with the Holy Spirit, may have a big surprise in store. But such a surprise should not be surprising, since it has happened so many times before.

It becomes increasingly evident, however, that talk about finding "another John Paul" needs to be discouraged. That possibility is nowhere in sight. As important as the pope is, the Church is ever so much larger than the pope. Interviewers ask about "the policies" of the next pope, as though each pontificate reinvents Catholicism. In fact, the papal office is very limited. Among the titles of the pope is *Servus servorum Dei*; he is the "servant of the servants of God," and his paramount service is to preserve and protect "the faith once delivered to the saints."

Am I suggesting that we brace ourselves for a pope who is in important respects less personally impressive than Karol Wojtyla? But of course. We have been graced to live in a time when a spiritual, intellectual, and pastoral giant walked the earth. The new pope will undoubtedly bring his distinctive gifts to the office. Most important, he will possess the gifts of authority and charism that come with the office.

Amidst all the chatter about the outcome of the conclave, it seems some here are forgetting that this is still the
week of mourning for the loss of John Paul II. We must not
allow last Friday's unprecedented manifestation of grief
and gratitude to be consigned to the news-cycle dustbin. I
will try to make that point in this evening's broadcast, for
which I am now running late. Last night I couldn't get a
taxi and it was a tough walk with my back acting up again.

Friday, April 15. Raymond and I had Fr. Peter Gumpel on
the EWTN broadcast last night. We thought that would
make for an interesting ten-minute segment, but it turned
into an utterly fascinating half hour.

Gumpel is from an aristocratic Austrian family and has
had personal encounters with popes going back to Pius XI. A
"relator" (an independent judge) in the office dealing with
the causes of saints, the Jesuit Gumpel has been working in
Rome for more than fifty years. Although he believes that
John Paul II will be, and should be, declared a saint, he is
strongly opposed to rushing the process. The procedures established in the sixteenth century—including the rigorous
examination of alleged miracles by the best medical science
of the times—is essential, he insists, to avoid the awkwardness of the subsequent discovery of possibly embarrassing
facts. He is also cool to the idea of declaring the late pope
"John Paul the Great," although there is no official procedure
for applying that title. "Does it mean that other popes were
not so great?" he asks. To which I counter, "Does declaring
him a saint mean that other popes were not so saintly?" We
agree to disagree on the appellation "John Paul the Great."

Of the 264 popes, 78 have been declared saints, many of them martyrs in the early centuries. The comparative merits of popes is always a subject of lively debate, as is evident in, for instance, Eamon Duffy's popular history of the popes, *Saints and Sinners.* In endless conversations this week about carrying on "the legacy of John Paul II," there is frequent discussion of whether the pope to be elected next week should take the title of "John Paul III." Doing that might set him up for unfair and invidious comparisons. It would be a good thing, it seems to me, if he reached back farther into history for a name. Aside from the comparison with John Paul II, "John Paul III" would reinforce the impression of some that the Church started with the period following the Second Vatican Council.

The practice of adopting a new name upon election goes back to the sixth century when a priest named Mercury was elected pope. It would never do to have a pope with such a blatantly pagan name, so he called himself John. Since then, the most popular names chosen by popes are, in order: John, Gregory, Benedict, Clement, Leo, Innocent, and Pius. Should Joseph Ratzinger be elected, I would not be surprised if he chose the name Boniface, the apostle to the Germans. On the other hand, Boniface was not himself a German, never mind a Bavarian.

At this writing, Ratzinger is, according to the rumor mills, in the lead, with forty or fifty electors indicating their support. The main mills are run by the Italian newspapers, and especially by *Corriere della Sera.* It is reluctantly admitted by other reporters that the Italian papers have the edge in getting inside information, the claim being that they are on the good side of a talkative cardinal or two.

According to Dublin bookmakers, the odds favor Lustiger of Paris and Martini, formerly of Milan, but nobody here in Rome gives their prospects much credence. One Italian daily is puffing Angelo Sodano, secretary of state under John Paul, as Ratzinger's chief rival; but that, too, is viewed as highly improbable. Yet another Italian daily claims the American cardinals are forming a bloc in opposition to Ratzinger, but I find that hard to credit; in recent years the American cardinals have not formed a bloc on much of anything, and at least a couple of them are great admirers of Ratzinger. Yesterday, one cardinal said the meetings are "tranquil and cordial," but another described the cardinals as "divided and gravely concerned." Take your pick. I imagine the Holy Spirit is amused by the confusion of tongues.

All that is going on here, this way of selecting a pope, is criticized in some circles for being antiquated, secretive, and undemocratic. There is something to that, but then one must ask what would be a better way. Some who are identified as champions of collegiality have proposed that there should be a worldwide consultation of the 4,000 bishops of the Church, including provisions for the contributions of priests and the lay faithful. One can imagine the nightmare of having a three- or six-month campaign season upon the death or retirement of a pope. Presumably the cardinals would be something like the electoral college in the American system, with each casting a vote in accord with the expressed wishes of his region. Such proposals are, in addition to being unworkable, a formula for unbridled politicking and factionalism.

The present procedure is to gather the cardinals, who are the senior bishops of the universal Church and chief consultants to the late pope, for a few days of prayer and getting to know one another, followed by a conclave in which, protected from the media and outside influences, they elect one of their own whom they trust to lead the Church for undetermined years into the future. People who are put off by the inevitable maneuverings and counter-maneuverings are lacking a Catholic and incarnational sensibility that is not offended by God's use of very human means to achieve His purposes. This does not mean that a bad pope cannot be elected. There have been more than a few bad popes. The promise is, as Cardinal Ratzinger said a couple of months ago, that nobody will be elected who will be able to destroy the Church or betray what Catholics call the deposit of faith. And maybe, please God, he will be another saint.

It is a cliché to say that the Church is not a democracy, but it is a cliché because so many recognize that it is true. There is always the danger of the arrogance and abuse of power, and patterns of consultation and collaboration can always be improved. But those who claimed after the Second Vatican Council that the Church's affirmation of democracy in the secular realm required, for the sake of consistency, the extension of democracy in the governance of the Church were wrong—and they are still wrong. The political sovereign in the temporal and temporary realm is "we the people." By way of sharpest contrast,

Christ is the sovereign of the Church. Of course, if Christ is Lord, he is Lord of all, but only in the Church is his sovereignty institutionalized, so to speak. In everything, and certainly in the choosing of a successor to Peter, the goal is to discern the will of Christ. And that I have no doubt is what is happening—not *despite* everything, but *through* everything—during these days in Rome.

Another thing or two before I leave for this evening's broadcast. On our EWTN broadcast, Fr. Peter Gumpel was especially appreciative of the work of Ronald Rychlak, Joseph Bottum, David Dalin, and others who have written in *First Things* in response to the many libelous attacks on Pius XII, such as John Cornwell's vulgar and dishonest book, *Hitler's Pope.* Gumpel spoke movingly of meetings with John Paul in which the late pope expressed his fervent hope that he would live long enough to beatify his esteemed predecessor, Pius XII. That was not to be, but Fr. Gumpel is confident Pius will be beatified in due course.

And then a word about those millions of people, mainly young people, who came to the funeral last Friday. I have not only seen several accounts of the "rock star" attraction of John Paul but also listened to worldly wise reporters describe it. In fact, the crowds, stretching more than three miles beyond St. Peter's, were wondrously solemn and prayerful. The Legionaries of Christ and other religious orders posted priests all along the way and there was a brisk business in confessions around the clock. One Legionary priest tells me of his nonstop hearing of confessions—from five o'clock in the afternoon until six o'clock the next morning. The mayor of Rome said that not one

225

serious crime was reported in the city during those days. That is hard to believe, but that is what he said.

John Paul went to the world and the world came to him, and they knew why they had come.

Monday, April 18. At the moment, at this very moment of writing, my dominant thought and feeling is far from edifying. This wretched laptop computer lost all 2,000 words of today's dispatch, and the technological wizards of EWTN have not been able to retrieve them.

As John Calvin is said to have said upon delivering a book to the printer, "It is very much like dropping a beautiful rose down a very deep well, never to be heard of again." That was centuries ago, and he had the satisfaction of knowing that determined folk would be able to find a copy. Not so in this age of digital revolution, and digital frustration. But enough. By an act of near-heroic self-discipline, I banish distracting outrage and set about reconstructing at least a digest of what seems worthy of report.

A few hours ago, the Sistine Chapel was hermetically sealed, or as hermetically sealed as anything can be in a world of high-tech communications, as a journalist described the world upon the laying of the first transatlantic telegraphic cable in 1858 or thereabouts. There is something deliciously satisfying in watching the more than 6,000 reporters accredited to these events, along with their hundreds of satellite trucks and anchorpersons at the ready, being forced to watch a stovepipe for a puff of smoke.

Interviewers incessantly complain about the secretiveness of it all; they argue that the public has a right to know, meaning that reporters should know what is happening so that they can tell the cardinals what the public is demanding. It is not entirely clear to some of us why CBS or the *New York Times* should have a say in selecting the Supreme Pontiff of the Catholic Church. Especially since they and others in the news industry do not really seem to have at heart the well-being of the Church and her mission. It is, in a somewhat perverse way, flattering that they think Catholicism is not just for Catholics, and, in a deep theological sense to which few of them are attuned, they are right about that.

What we are witnessing is the assertion of the Church's identity as a distinct and apostolically constituted society that insists upon governing itself. This is known as the *libertas ecclesiae*—the freedom of the Church. Particularly delightful are the solemn prayers and oaths at the beginning of the conclave in which electors are required to eschew influence by temporal principalities and powers in the outcome. It was not so long ago, as the Church marks time, that Spain, France, and the Austro-Hungarian empire claimed, and sometimes exercised, the right to veto papal candidates. One cannot imagine Jacques Chirac or, for that matter, George W. Bush trying to interfere in this election.

It is certainly not that the Church has become less important in the contemporary world, as is evident in the events of these past two weeks. It is, rather, a mark of the Church's confidence in her freedom to order her life according to the truths by which she was created and is sustained. Meanwhile, the media's delusions of omnipotence are put on hold as thousands of journalists are reduced to watching a stovepipe, and a rather rickety-looking one at that.

Now this writing is interrupted by the sad news that Diane Knippers has died. The cancer seemed to be in remission this past year or so, but then it came back with a vengeance. Diane was the formidable head of the Institute on Religion and Democracy, based in Washington, D.C., which I had a hand in launching in 1981.

The Institute on Religion and Democracy played a powerful role in contending for a recovery of an approximation of orthodoxy in the mainline/oldline liberal churches of American Protestantism. Some thought it a futile effort, but no fair-minded person denied its nobility.

The connection with what is happening here may not be obvious to everyone, but Diane and the Institute on Religion and Democracy are of a piece with the orthodox insurgencies that have brought us a significant distance from where the Christian communities, or at least some of them, were twenty and thirty years ago. Then, and on every front, liberalism seemed to be on a roll. Among Catholics, the revolution mandated by "the spirit of Vatican II" appeared unstoppable to many.

Among the old unstoppables, few were so prominent as Father Richard McBrien of Notre Dame. I apologize for mentioning him again, but he is irresistible. He was trotted out again this morning for a column in the *International Herald Tribune*. He opined that all of the *papabili* are distressingly indifferent to the alienation of major constituencies of the Church—gay activists, proponents of women's ordination, and what he described as the more liberal "middle-aged and elderly clergy." What would the Church be without them? We can only try to imagine. A few days ago, the same Fr. McBrien was on the tube complaining about the regressive influence of John Paul II. Finally, the interviewer asked whether he was not impressed by the 4 or 5 million people, most of them young people, who came to the funeral. Not at all, he replied. Those, he explained, were the young people the Church already had. What about the millions who did not show up?

To such cantankerousness are the old unstoppables now reduced. But I digress. Diane did her part, and more than her part, in persuasively proposing that the future belongs to the friends of fidelity. May choirs of angels welcome her on the far side of Jordan.

Tuesday, April 19. Yesterday, there was an exultant cry from the crowds in St. Peter's Square when for the first few seconds the smoke appeared to be white. Historians say there hasn't been a first-ballot election for centuries, not since the days when popes were elected by acclamation or installed by Medici bribery or put on the throne at the point of the secular sword. Had there been a decision yesterday, or if there is one in the ballots of today (two in the morning, two in the afternoon), Joseph Ratzinger would almost certainly be pope.

I have over these days been out on a limb, saying that Ratzinger will be elected on the second day of balloting. My assumption is that he is the only cardinal who went into the conclave within reach of the two-thirds (seventy-seven votes) necessary for election.

There is dispute about whether he hurt himself with his homily at the beginning of the conclave. Another interpretation is that he deliberately set a dour tone to reduce the prospect of his being elected; the premise being that he will accept but does not want the office. He said, among other things:

How many winds of doctrine we have known in recent decades, how many ideological currents, how many ways of thinking. . . . The small boat of thought of many Christians has often been tossed about by these waves—thrown from one extreme to the other: from Marxism to liberalism, even to libertinism; from collectivism to radical individualism; from atheism to a vague religious mysticism; from agnosticism to syncretism, and so forth. Every day new sects are created and what Saint Paul says about human trickery comes true, with cunning which tries to draw those into error (cf. Ephesians 4:14). Having a clear faith, based on the Creed of the Church, is often labeled today as a fundamentalism. Whereas, relativism, which is letting oneself be tossed and "swept along by every wind of teaching," looks like the only attitude acceptable to today's standards. We are moving towards a dictatorship of relativism which does not recognize anything as for certain and which has as its highest goal one's own ego and one's own desires.

The phrase "dictatorship of relativism" made all the headlines. There might be something to the speculation that he is deliberately dampening support for his election. It is no secret that he earnestly desires to return to his work as an academic theologian; indeed, he acceded to John Paul's desire that he head up the Doctrine of the Faith very reluctantly and only under obedience. He tried to resign in 1991, in 1996, and again in 2001. But, as he has described it, when he saw the determined obedience of the frail John Paul II in continuing until the end, he could not bring himself to insist upon resigning.

I would not be surprised if the headlines are already written announcing the election of the reactionary, arch-conservative, doctrinal enforcer Joseph Ratzinger. In fact, the "controversial" homily was a call for an "adult faith" that rejected the "extremes" of agnosticism or fundamentalism, of relentless skepticism or credulous fideism. Amid all the pomp and glory and media hype, Ratzinger reminded the cardinals that apart from Jesus Christ it all means exactly nothing. Challenging the liberal vs. conservative dichotomy that is the staple of the comic-strip caricatures offered by media chatter, he insisted that love without truth is blind, and truth without love is—and here he quoted 1 Corinthians 13—but a clanging cymbal.

I have known the man for more than twenty years; during this time we have had many occasions to discuss many things, and the homily was Ratzinger straight: precise, intense, radically Christocentric, and marked by a tranquil and humble obedience to the truth. Commenting on the words of the Lord, namely that the disciples are not servants but friends, Ratzinger ended on the winsome note, "Thank you, Jesus, for your friendship."

The conservative-moderate-liberal template that dominates reporting here in Rome is nonsense. There are different personalities and competencies among the cardinals, along with different views of how the Curia should operate in maintaining a center in a universal Church with powerful centrifugal dynamics. But on the issues with which many are obsessed, discernible differences among the cardinals are either slight or nonexistent, or at least among the cardinals given any chance of being elected.

A substantive question relative to Ratzinger's possible election is that he would like to restore the Congregation for the Doctrine of the Faith to its position of undoubted preeminence in the Curia, a position that Paul VI's curial reforms resulted in giving to the Secretariat of State. The idea is that doctrine and theology should have priority over diplomacy and politics in the Church's governance.

But now they are calling us back to our broadcasting perch atop the North American College. It is Tuesday afternoon and, after two black smokes, we are expecting another two votes. There is good precedent for the third balloting to be decisive. By the time you read this you may well know more than I or anybody here, apart from the cardinal electors, knows about who will be the 264th successor to Peter. Or maybe not.

Wednesday, April 20. At about 5:50 last evening, the smoke appeared again. Raymond and I—along with, I expect, half the population of the world—couldn't make out whether it was black or white. It appeared to be gray, but there is no canonical provision for gray smoke. (At a festive dinner last night at the Taverna Julia, the word was that the cardinals had problems with the chemicals to be put into the Sistine Chapel stove. None of them has had much experience with this sort of thing.) We had been alerted to the provision that, in addition to the white smoke, the bells of St. Peter's would ring if there had been an election. We excitedly went back and forth on the color of the smoke, which continued to be gray; but then a bell of St. Peter's began ringing. Was this it? No, it was only the clock bell announcing the hour. But within minutes the smoke turned decidedly white. There was no doubt about it. And then the bells began to ring; first those of St. Peter's and then the bells of all the churches of Rome. But who is it?

I'm rather sure it's Ratzinger, I told our viewers, evincing a confidence that was in large part hope. We did not have long to wait. A little more than a half hour later, the appointed cardinal messenger appeared on the loggio and declared: "*Annuntio vobis gaudium magnum; habemus Papam: Eminentissimum ac Reverendissimum Dominum, Dominum Josephum . . .* " At the name "Josephum," exultant cheers broke out from the crowd. There was no other Joseph in contention, it had to be him. The announcement continued: "*Sanctae Romanae Ecclesiae Cardinalem Ratzinger qui sibi nomen imposuit Benedictum XVI.*" "I announce to you news of great joy: We have a Pope. The most eminent and reverend lord Joseph of the holy Roman Church, Cardinal Ratzinger who has taken the name Benedict XVI." Then the crowd of hundreds of thousands, if not millions, filling St. Peter's Square and stretching down the

Via Della Conciliazione, across the Tiber, and into the side streets of Rome, went wild.

Habemus Papam. Ratzinger. Benedict XVI. Deo gratias. Or, as this American put it: How sweet it is.

Thursday, April 21. Within hours of the announcement *Habemus Papam* from the loggia of St. Peter's, those who have for years viewed Joseph Ratzinger as the embodiment of all they think is wrong with the Church were publicly exhibiting (to paraphrase Winston Churchill) magnanimity in defeat. Led by Hans Küng, Ratzinger's self-anointed nemesis, they proposed that Ratzinger should be given a grace period, perhaps a hundred days, to demonstrate that he has repented of his reactionary ways.

The responsibilities of his old work, as prefect of the Congregation for the Doctrine of the Faith, and the responsibilities of his new work, as pope, are significantly different. The pope, it is rightly said, must strive to be the father (as in "pope") of all the faithful—which is a challenge for him but a greater challenge to those who are dubiously faithful.

With the election of Pope Benedict XVI, the curtain has fallen on the long-running drama of "the spirit of Vatican II," the myth in which the revolution mandated by the Council was delayed by the timidity of Paul VI and temporarily derailed for twenty-six years by the regressive John Paul II as the Church inexorably moved toward the happy denouement of "the next pope," a leader who would resume the course of progressive accommodation to the wisdom of the modern world. The curtain has fallen and the audience has long since left, except for a few diehards who say they are giving the new management a hundred days to revive the show. Some of them are perhaps thinking of going to another theater. There are worse things than not being a Catholic—when it becomes unmistakably clear that being a Catholic is not what one is.

I very much doubt that Pope Benedict is going to engage in wholesale excommunications, but I have no doubt that he will encourage people to ponder anew what is entailed in being in communion with the Church. He has over the years made evident that he believes we are engaged in a great battle for the soul of Western civilization and, indeed, the soul of the world. Much has been made of the supposed contrast between John Paul II's confident expectation of a "springtime of evangelization" and Joseph Ratzinger's frequent references to a smaller but more faithful Church which has internalized the words of Jesus that the seed must fall into the ground and die before it can bear much fruit. In this account, John Paul the ebullient is to be contrasted with Ratzinger the dour.

There is a measure of truth in that contrast. Some of it is related to differences in personality, some of it to differences in intellectual formation. Avery Cardinal Dulles summarized the witness of John Paul in the phrase "prophetic humanism." The Ratzinger of the past gave voice to a more explicit and insistent Christocentric humanism, and the Benedict of the future, will, I expect, continue to do so.

This is not to say that John Paul was not Christocentric. There were few passages from the Council that he quoted

235

more often than the declaration from *Gaudium et Spes* that Jesus Christ is not only the revelation of God to man but the revelation of man to himself. The suggested contrast between John Paul and Benedict is not a disagreement, but Ratzinger's accent has been more explicitly on the crucified Christ and the necessarily cruciform experience of the Church through time.

It has been suggested that the different accents may reflect the fact that Ratzinger is more Augustinian in his theology while John Paul was more of a Thomist. Both accents issue in the bold admonition, "Be not afraid." That signature phrase of John Paul has been emphatically repeated by Benedict XVI. The crucified Christ is the risen and victorious Christ who, in a favorite passage of Ratzinger's, tells the disciples, "Fear not, little flock, it is the Father's good pleasure to give to you the kingdom." With an emphasis on the *little* in the little flock.

From his copious writings as Ratzinger, we know that Benedict is robustly skeptical of sociological depictions and analyses of the Church. The general media, as well as many scholars, are obsessed with statistical assessments of the Church's fortunes and misfortunes in history. For Pope Benedict, these assessments are almost beside the point. The media will have a hard time adjusting to this. They do not want to talk about revealed truth or the redemption worked by Jesus Christ. Benedict insists that to speak of the Church is to speak of Christ. Which may result in the secular elite's declining to talk about either.

The circumstance was nicely summed up by a comment of Ted Koppel on ABC's *Nightline* the night of the election. The subject turned to interreligious dialogue, and I had referred to the radical Christocentrism of the new pope. "So which is it, Father," Koppel asked, "Christ or interreligious dialogue?"

But, of course, it is interreligious dialogue because of, and upon the foundation of, Jesus Christ who is the redeemer of the entire world, including the world's religions in which, as Catholic teaching holds, elements of truth and grace are to be found. The same confusion arises with respect to *Dominus Iesus,* a document issued by Ratzinger's Congregation for the Doctrine of the Faith in 2000, which is regularly cited as claiming that Catholicism is more true than other religions and even other Christian churches. But of course. There is but one Christ and therefore, at the deep level of theological understanding, there can be only one Church, and the Catholic Church claims to be that Church most fully and rightly ordered through time. That is not in tension with ecumenism; it is the foundation of the ecumenical quest for full communion among all Christians.

The argument that Ratzinger has tried to make through these many years, and the argument that Benedict will undoubtedly be making, is that there is no tension, never mind conflict, between truth and love. The caricature is that liberals are big on love, conservatives are big on truth. As Ratzinger said in his homily before the conclave, love without truth is blind and truth without love is empty. Without truth, love is mere sentimentality and, without love, truth is sterile.

This is, of course, in perfect continuity with John Paul's favored passage from *Gaudium et Spes* that Christ—who is the way, the truth, and the life—is the revelation of man to himself. If Christ is the truth about everyone and every thing, then the way forward is by following the way of Christ. This is the genuine progressivism proposed to the Church and the world by John Paul and by Benedict. The Church does not seek to be countercultural, but it is unavoidably counter to the modern mindset in proposing that fidelity and continuity, not autonomy and novelty, are the paths toward a more promising future.

Within the continuing tradition, the Second Vatican Council is an extraordinary moment of development and refinement. Among the many achievements of the pontificate of John Paul the Great, some would say the *most* important achievement, was to secure the hermeneutic for the interpretation of that great council. Joseph Ratzinger was an invaluable partner in that achievement, and the partner has now become the heir who will build upon that achievement.

The day of his election was, in the calendar of the Church, the day of Leo IX, the eleventh-century pope who energetically used the papacy to advance the spiritual renewal of Europe, and of Germany in particular. Ratzinger is more a Bavarian than a German, Bavaria having a distinct identity that goes back long before the Prussian invention of modern Germany in the nineteenth century. But I expect he sees some striking parallels between the eleventh-century reign of Leo and the needs of our time. Which is, once again, to recognize the bond with the first Benedict, who set out to reconstruct, beginning with the Church, a civilization that had fallen into ruins. The new pope's most determined opponents will be those who, in the words of St. Paul, boast of their shame and demand that the Church not only acquiesce in but give her blessing to the devastations conventionally called progress. As Ratzinger forcefully argued, the achievements of modernity, which are considerable, are fragile and prone to self-destruction unless grounded in the truth; and the truth, ultimately, is the Son of God who, as St. John puts it, was sent not to condemn the world but to save the world (John 3:17).

Pope Benedict XVI is seventy-eight years old, and some speak of a brief transitional pontificate. I do not expect it will be brief, and I am sure it will not be transitional, if transitional means a holding action until the next pontificate. Benedict has definite views on what needs to be reformed in the Church, including much that in recent decades was called reform, and he will in his self-effacing but determined way press for changes in the service of a continuity that has too often been recklessly violated.

In this respect, he will be carrying forward the work of John Paul the Great in bringing together again the great themes of the Second Vatican Council: *ressourcement* and *aggiornamento*. The reappropriation of the tradition and the conversation with the contemporary world are not two agendas, one dubbed conservative and the other liberal, but the two essential dimensions of the renewal of the Church.

And, if the Council is right in saying that the Church is the sacrament of the world, the renewal of the Church is the way toward the renewal of the world, as the first Benedict believed and so powerfully demonstrated.

We are now well into the pontificate of Benedict XVI and, reading once more the above reflections written during the momentous days of April 2005, there is little I would change. Benedict has moved aggressively on the ecumenical front. There are signs that, just maybe, the Orthodox will be more responsive to his overtures than they were to those of John Paul. Social scientists speak of a "propinquity paradox," meaning that kinship breeds suspicion rather than trust. John Paul was a Slav, and the long and troubled (to put it very gently) history of conflict between Poland and Russia may have made it more, not less, difficult for his fellow Slavs to fully credit his initiatives. It might be that the Russians in particular and the Orthodox more generally will feel less threatened in working with a pope more clearly "from the West." The word in Rome is that the papal visit to Russia, which John Paul sought in vain, may now soon happen.

Early on, Benedict took up the theme of evangelization in a way reminiscent of John Paul's statement in *Redemptoris Missio* (The Mission of the Redeemer) that the Church imposes nothing, she only proposes. There are those, Benedict observed, who say that non-Christians should be "left in peace" out of respect for their own "authentic" beliefs, whatever they may be. "But how can this be the case," asked Benedict, "if the true authenticity of every person is found in communion with Christ and not without him? Isn't it our duty to offer them this essential reality?"

As Joseph Ratzinger did in his many writings, so Benedict has emphatically underscored the unbreakable connection between freedom and truth. The truth of Christ does not restrict, never mind abolish, freedom, but is the foundation of freedom. Already at the Mass of Installation on April 24, he said, "If we let Christ enter fully into our lives, if we open ourselves totally to him, are we not afraid that he might take something away from us?" He answered, "No! If we let Christ into our lives, we lose nothing, nothing, absolutely nothing of what makes life free, beautiful, and great. . . . Only in this friendship is the great potential of human existence truly revealed. Only in this friendship do we experience beauty and liberation."

Contrary to the general assumption, the church of St. John Lateran, not St. Peter's, is the Pope's cathedral in Rome. There on May 7 Benedict spoke about the nature of the office he has assumed: "The power conferred by Christ to Peter and his successors is, in an absolute sense, a mandate for service. . . . The power to teach in the Church implies a commitment to service in obedience to the faith. The Pope is not an absolute sovereign whose thoughts and desire are the law." In several statements and ceremonial actions, he seemed to signal that he intended to maintain a lower profile than did John Paul. He has given renewed prominence to the title of the Pope as *servus servorum Dei*—the servant of the servants of God.

Despite claims to the contrary, Benedict is a great champion of episcopal collegiality. Over the years he has been critical of the operations of national episcopal conferences precisely because their bureaucracies too often stifle the responsibility of bishops to be the teachers of the faith in their local churches, meaning the diocese. The role of Peter in the Church is to "strengthen the brethren" (Luke 22) in the doing of what they are ordained to do. Bishops should be bishops, not managers of a local franchise granted by the national bishops conference or, for that matter, by Rome.

From the very beginning, at the Mass of Installation, Benedict struck another note. Over the years, the worry had been expressed, usually sotto voce, that John Paul, with his deep and distinctive philosophical-theological formation, had put too much of a personal imprint on magisterial teaching. And now the Church has another pope who is a high-powered intellectual. As though to anticipate the same worry about his pontificate, Benedict assured the college of bishops, "My real program of governance is not to do my own will, not to pursue my own ideas, but to listen, together with the whole church, to the word and the will of the Lord."

Although it is often forgotten, during Benedict's more than twenty years at the Congregation for the Doctrine of the Faith, few theologians were formally censured. He has great respect for the theologian's task to inquire, explore, and suggest ways in which the Church can better preserve and communicate the truth with which she is entrusted. The only condition is that such inquiring, exploring, and suggesting be in the service of—to use one of his favored phrases—"the structure of faith."

Along with many others who have known him, and known him better than I, I can testify to Pope Benedict XVI's serenity of soul and gentleness of manner. It would be a serious error, however, to mistake that serenity and gentleness for weakness or lack of firm resolve. This will be, I am persuaded, not a transitional but a transformative papacy.

Coming to the end of this reflection on Catholic matters, I am keenly aware of having tried to say so much, and yet I have said such a small part of it. Chesterton was right: The Church is so much larger from the inside than from the outside. My boyhood intuition is confirmed again and again: Catholicism is *more*. And I wonder about the subtitle, *Confusion, Controversy, and the Splendor of Truth*. I have addressed confusion and controversy in considerable detail, but have I said enough about the splendor of truth? Have I made it sufficiently evident that every No spoken by the Church is but an entailment of an immeasurably greater Yes? As she is large, encompassing the whole of the human condition, so she is generous, patient, and long-suffering. Little wonder that she is called Holy Mother. But even if I had written a much bigger and better book about Catholic matters, it would have been only a very small part of it.

To get a feel for The Catholic Thing, the theologians, spiritual writers, and popes are necessary, but one must also go to the poets, novelists, and writers of short stories. That is where the "analogical imagination" of Catholicism is on exuberant display. The canon is rich and long: Flannery O'Connor, Walker Percy, Allen Tate, Thomas Merton, J. F. Powers, Edwin O'Connor, Georges Bernanos, J.R.R. Tolkien, Dorothy Day, Evelyn Waugh, and on and on. Recent history, one wag has observed, has been more productive of ex-Catholic writers, and there is something to that. But whether they are faithful, lapsed, or altogether collapsed, their imaginations are informed by The Catholic Thing.

What makes all these writers Catholic, aside from their being Catholics, is the palpable assumption—sometimes quiet and sometimes shouted—that being Catholic is a different way of being in the world. The sense is nicely caught in the title of Flannery O'Connor's collected letters, *The Habit of Being*. Catholicism is not a theological construction, and certainly not the construction of a school of brilliant intellectuals. It is not a code of moral rules or an institutional supplier of spiritual uplift. One cannot begin to understand it without theology; moral rules mark the path to the holiness to which we are called, and

Catholicism offers a spiritual alternative to the world's abandonment to nihilism and despair. But, mainly, Catholicism is a habit of being in the centuries-long company of those, living and dead, who are part of a distinctive society with its own memories, vocabulary, rituals, devotions, and, yes, confusions and controversies, that are necessarily part of living in the splendor of the truth who is Jesus Christ.

I have by no means mastered the habit of being Catholic. Nobody has. That's part of being Catholic. Had I another hundred years to live, I would still be a little boy wandering around—with awe and curiosity and frequent surprise, both of delight and scandal—the capacious home that is Catholicism. Remembering that there is but one Christ and therefore but one Church, it is the Church into which I was baptized so long ago at St. John's Lutheran in Pembroke, Ontario. The story of my entering into full communion, which was the remedying of an imperfect communion, is not typical. But again, whose is?

My years as a Catholic have also been somewhat curious. In part because of the work I have been given to do, and also because of contingencies such as friendships. All, encompassed by providential direction, is contingency. In 1997, John Paul the Great appointed me a delegate to a synod in Rome. On the concluding day of the synod, I was seated at lunch between John Cardinal O'Connor and Joseph Cardinal Ratzinger. In the midst of lively conversation about many things, I was suddenly moved to say how grateful I was that I had come into the Church at a time when I could have John O'Connor as my bishop and Joseph Ratzinger heading the Church's office of doctrine. They were a bit embarrassed by my outburst, as was I, but it seemed like the thing to say at the moment. Some months later, I related that conversation to John Paul. He smiled in his mischievous way and said, "So, you are not grateful for your pope?"

I mention the incident, at the risk of unseemly name-dropping, because I sense my remaining years will be different. Remember Newman's remark that he was happiest in the barque of Peter when he was not near the engine room, meaning the Church's leadership and the Holy See in particular. I have no delusions about having influenced what happened in the engine room, but I was close to some of those who did. As pleased as I was when Joseph Ratzinger became Pope Benedict, upon the death of John Paul the Great I had the sense that "my pontificate" was over. The reader will have recognized the presence John Paul II in almost every page of this book.

I was hardly young, but during those twenty-six years of his reign the lines of Wordsworth frequently came to mind:

> *Bliss was it in that dawn to be alive,*
> *But to be young was very heaven!*

Much has been written about John Paul's "style"—his ebullience, his energy, his hopefulness, his engagement with young people, his courage in suffering, his grace in dying as he lived. For generations yet unborn, all that will likely be the stuff of legends. All that is also inextricably tied to John Paul the teacher, an aspect of his pontificate that is, or so it seems to me, not fully appreciated. Sometimes it seemed we were getting an encyclical per month, each one bringing alive Scripture, centuries of living tradition, and especially the Second Vatican Council to display new dimensions of the splendor of the truth.

There is, for instance, *Centesimus Annus* (The Hundredth Year), which is, bar none, the most comprehensive, coherent, and compelling depiction of the free, just, and democratic society available to the modern world. *Ut Unum Sint* (That They May Be One) wondrously clarified the gift of Christian unity, and the ecumenical task of which we must never weary. *Evangelium Vitae* (The Gospel of Life) helped the world to understand its choice between the culture of life and the culture of death, and is the magna carta of a pro-life movement that must continue until the end of time. And then there is *Veritatis Splendor* (The Splendor of Truth), persuading us to believe that there is moral truth, and proposing a more excellent way to a world that is dying from, in the fine phrase of Orthodox theologian David Hart, metaphysical boredom.

Such teaching documents and so many other initiatives made the pontificate of John Paul "my pontificate." And yet, in the midst of the wrenching sense of loss, there was the awareness that he and his pontificate were but one luminous moment in the long story of the Church. I said that I expect the pontificate of Benedict to be not transitional but transformative. I have no doubt that important to that transformation will be Benedict's efforts to advance and develop the initiatives of John Paul. The truth is that the teaching initiatives of John Paul have not been received and internalized by the great majority of bishops, theologians, and priests, never mind by the Catholic people.

Benedict will introduce initiatives of his own. He is a man of extraordinary wisdom and intellect, and he enjoys a striking ability to communicate the faith in a winsome manner. It is likely that the millions of people, especially young people, who called themselves "John Paul II Catholics" will soon be saying they are "Benedict Catholics." This continuity of devotion was already dramatically evident at Benedict's first World Youth Day in Cologne, Germany, in the summer of 2005. One observer remarked that Cologne shows that the "personality cult" is transferable, but that is quite entirely to miss the point. Rather, these young people know, as all of us should know, that the habit of being Catholic is inseparable from Peter among us. A pope is not the Church but he is, under Christ and with the tattered apostolic band of bishops, the center that holds the pilgrimage together through time to the promised End Time.

I am frequently asked whether I still stand by the hopeful vision set out in my 1987 book, *The Catholic Moment*. The answer is unqualifiedly yes. If the Catholic Church is what she claims to be, and I am convinced that she is, then every moment from Pentecost to the coming of the promised Kingdom is the Catholic moment. Despite the unfaithfulness of many, including bishops, popes, and Catholics beyond numbering, Christ is faithful. From the assurance of the risen Lord to Peter and the frightened disciples by the Sea of Galilee to the election of John Paul in October 1978 and of Benedict in April 2005, his word is sure: "Be not afraid." The center holds. The adventure continues.

It happened again this morning. At my working-class parish of Immaculate Conception at First Avenue and Fourteenth Street in Manhattan. The older Italians and Irish, the younger blacks and Hispanics, along with the preternaturally devout Filipinos who are almost a third of the parish. The familiar ritual, the familiar words, and Christ did it again, just as he said he would. *Ex opere operato*, as Catholics say. It is the Mass that holds the Church together, which is to say it is Christ truly present in the Mass. It will continue to happen until he returns in glory.

At the conclusion of the Our Father, the priest prays:

Deliver us, Lord, from every evil, and grant us peace in our day. In your mercy keep us free from sin and protect us from all anxiety as we wait in joyful hope for the coming of our Savior, Jesus Christ.

And always those words of the third eucharistic prayer, appealing to the splendor of truth in the midst of the sins and anxieties of our confusions and controversies:

Strengthen in faith and love your pilgrim Church on earth.

Notes

Chapter 1

1. The strange history of the mistelling of the Scopes trial is nicely summarized by Carol Iannone in "The Truth About *Inherit the Wind*," *First Things*, no. 70 (February 1997): 28–33. The continuing, and perhaps increasing, popularity of *Inherit the Wind* in public schools may reflect a growing fear in some circles of the ascendancy of "the religious right" in American public life.

2. Mark Noll of Wheaton College is the premier historian of evangelicalism. See his *The Old Religion in a New World: The History of North American Christianity* (Wm. B. Eerdmans Publishing Company, 2001).

3. See Benton Johnson, Dean R. Hoge, and Donald A. Luidens on Presbyterian adherence in "Mainline Churches: The Real Reason for Decline," *First Things*, no. 31 (March 1993): 13–18.

4. For a readable and non-Catholic account of the early Church, see Williston Walker et al., *A History of the Christian Church*, 4th ed. (Scribner, 1985). For a good account of the development of the papacy, see Eamon Duffy, *Saints and Sinners: A History of the Popes* (Yale University Press, 1997).

5. In the much writing about the distinction, see "subsists" and "is." Avery Dulles's *Catholicity of the Church & Structures of Catholicism* (Oxford University Press, 1995) is particularly helpful.

Chapter 2

1. Bonhoeffer sermon quoted in Eberhard Bethge, *Dietrich Bonhoeffer* (New York: Harper & Row, 1970), 42.

2. Jaroslav Pelikan, *The Riddle of Roman Catholicism* (Abingdon Press, 1959). Later in life, Pelikan entered into communion with the Orthodox Church in America.

Chapter 3

1. R. R. Reno, "Out of the Ruins," *First Things*, no. 150 (February 2005): 11–16.

2. Yves Congar, *The Meaning of Tradition* (Hawthorn Books, 1964).

Chapter 4

1. The formidable John Noonan has impressively campaigned for what he believes is greater candor in recognizing that church teaching changes rather than develops. For a valuable critique of Noonan's project, see Avery Cardinal Dulles on "John Noonan's Changing Church," *First Things* (October 2005).

Chapter 5

1. Quoted in Carol and Philip Zaleski, *Prayer: A History* (Houghton Mifflin, 2005), 131.

2. Eamon Duffy, "To Fast Again," *First Things*, no. 151 (March 2005): 4–9.

3. Mr. Archie Salerno of Florham Park, New Jersey, has generously given me permission to quote from his unpublished journal of a Catholic boyhood. I have taken the liberty of joining his reflections to those shared by other Catholics of the same era, resulting in a composite reflection I attribute to a fictional Archie Dinoia. I am grateful to Mr. Salerno for providing most of the material cited, and trust that he will approve of the result.

4. "You are the body of Christ." Perhaps a further word would be welcomed by those particularly interested in liturgical reforms and destablizations. Long before the Second Vatican Council, there was, as I mention in the text, a liturgical renewal among Catholics. It was in crucial respects very different from what is called liturgical reform today. In the 1950s, I was attracted to the movement under the auspices of the sainted Monsignor Martin Hellriegel of Holy Cross Church in St. Louis. Father Michael Mathis was another early pioneer, and the Center for Pastoral Liturgy at the University of Notre Dame gives out a Michael Mathis Award, which a few years ago went to Bishop Donald Trautman of Erie, Pennsylvania. Trautman was chairman of the bishops' liturgy committee in the 1990s and, to the surprise of many, was again elected to that position in 2004, an election that was taken as a direct protest against Rome's efforts to establish a greater measure of liturgical order. Receiving the Notre Dame award, Bishop Trautman launched a strident attack on critics of what has become the liturgical status quo, such as Joseph Cardinal Ratzinger, Msgr. Klaus Gamber, Fr. Joseph Fessio, and American groups such as Adoremus and CREDO. The tide is turning, Trautman declared, raising the question, "Is liturgical renewal becoming a dinosaur?" The critics say they want to "reform the reform," but Trautman does not credit their intentions for a moment. The proposals of the critics are "alarming." "They are indicative that the liturgical advances of Vatican II are in trouble—advances which the vast majority of Catholics have received positively." While asserting that the people like the changes, he also criticizes liturgists for failing to enlist the support of the people. "We have missed golden opportunities to reach the people in the pews," said the bishop. On a college campus he said he recently saw a tee-shirt displaying the message, "Join the resistance—support Vatican II." I have seen the same tee-shirt. The bishop took it as a message of support for the changes since Vatican II. The young woman wearing the tee-shirt I saw explained that she supports the understanding of Vatican II advanced by John Paul II and Cardinal Ratzinger and urges resistance against those who have wreaked change and confusion in the name of "the spirit of the Council." Obviously, there are major disagreements about the meaning of Vatican II. But it obviously is not obvious to Bishop Trautman, for whom any criticism of his version of the reform is an attack on the Council.

In his speech, Trautman repeatedly called for "full, conscious, and active participation" in the liturgy. A bishop of like mind announced a while back that, using a stopwatch, he calculated that for forty-four minutes of a Mass the people were not doing anything. Maybe they were praying or reflecting on the Word of God, which he clearly was not. But Bishop Trautman's particular passion is for "horizontal inclusive language" in Scripture readings and liturgy. Some readers may not be familiar with the terminology. As best I understand it, vertical language goes up and down, and horizontal language goes sideways. Bishop Trautman favors "moderate horizontal inclusive language," which sounds like a diagonal compromise. "I say to you," Trautman said at Notre Dame, "addressing women using male language denies women their own identity." No doubt some women have told him that, although a recent national survey, reinforced by pastoral experience, suggests that not only is there little popular support for what is called "inclusive" language but also considerable opposition to it. Here, too, it seems that those who presume to speak for "the people in the pews" are not in conversation with the people in the pews. The bishop has a point with the *Catechism of the Catholic Church*, which in its excessively literal translation ends up with an overuse of "man" and "men" that is simply bad English. He cites a *Catechism* passage that says priests should "give themselves entirely to God and to men." He comments, "Given homosexual behavior in our society, this is not the appropriate language to promote celibacy." A really keen sensitivity to sexual innuendo, one might suggest, would give the bishop pause about his enthusiasm for "horizontal" language regardless of gender. Panicked by the prospect that his cause could become a "dinosaur," the bishop seized upon any argument at hand. The possibility that people may think the *Catechism* is promoting homosexuality "is an example of why exclusive language is unacceptable." He also makes much of the fact that Tyndale, a Protestant publisher, recently put out an inclusive translation of the Bible. "If Bible scholars from the fundamentalist tradition . . . employ gender-inclusive language and our revised edition of the lectionary offers only a tokenism, there is a serious loss to God's people," said Bishop Trautman. "It is no secret that many Roman Catholics are entering fundamentalist churches today. How can the Roman Catholic tradition fail to keep pace even with the evangelical tradition in offering inclusive language?"

Even with those fundamentalists and evangelicals. How backward can we Catholics be? In his grasping for an argument, however, the bishop gets quite muddled. I do not want to believe for a minute that he believes that Catholics are becoming fundamentalists because they want gender-inclusive language. Fundamentalists are as enthusiastic about gender-inclusive language as Bishop Trautman is about the Tridentine Mass. The Tyndale experiment is a nonevent. The big development on the Bible translation front is that the publishers of the New International Version (NIV)—which is by far the most widely used translation among Protestants—recently announced that they are definitively shelving plans to dabble, even ever so cautiously, with inclusive language. The earlier suggestion that they might do so met with massive protests. If Catholics are becoming fundamentalists, it is more likely in order to escape the "reforms" promoted by Trautman and his likeminded reformers. He laments that the "reformers of the reform" now have the upper hand in the Church. "There is a dismantling of the renewal taking place before our very eyes," he declares. But then he offers the consolation that the reformers of an earlier day were also given a hard time, only to be vindicated later. "Why do we hurt our best and brightest?" he plaintively asks. Speaking of the best and brightest, he immediately adds, "By God's providence there are similarities between Father Mathis and myself." Ah, the lot of the unappreciated. A prophet is not without honor . . . Rome's proposed remedies of misguided reform imply that Bishop Trautman and others in the liturgical establishment made mistakes. This, he suggests, is outrageous, although it is taken as self-evident truth that Rome has for decades been making mistakes with predictable regularity. The liturgical guild's criticism of Rome is one thing. Rome's criticism of the liturgical guild—and even of some American bishops!—is quite another. In fact, there is much to approve in changes made since the Council. Although there are no doubt some who would like to, Catholics cannot and should not simply go back to the way things were. In his undiscriminating defense of the liturgical establishment, however, Bishop Trautman dismisses critics as reactionaries. There is a big difference, however, between antiquarianism and respect for tradition, continuity, and patterns of popular devotion. That earlier liturgical renewal was one of *ressourcement*, of reappropriating the fullness of the tradition in order to complement and, where necessary, correct liturgical practice ossified by mistaking mystification for mystery. That was the renewal embraced by Vatican II. Then came the agitations of those who mistook reform for perpetual innovation.

In the 1960s, I was the token Protestant on the board of the National Liturgical Conference. It once attracted 15,000 or more participants to its annual liturgical weeks. By the end of the sixties, the liturgical week (it may have been the last one) attracted a ragtag crowd of hippies manqué under the slogan of e. e. cummings's "damn everything but the circus." What passed for the avant garde of liturgical reform had become a disheveled and depressing circus of preening self-indulgence and uncritical celebration of everything in the cultural marketplace that presented itself as liberation from putatively stifling tradition.

Bishop Trautman cites the great liturgical scholar Josef Jungman in his support, but there is a great disjunction between Jungman's work and the liturgical establishment of today. Many of the pioneers, such as Martin Hellriegel, became vocal critics of the liturgical revolution, and for their troubles were derisively dismissed as oldtimers who had lost touch with "the spirit of the Council." In fact, and although they did not use the phrase, they were the first advocates of the "reform of the reform." After thirty years of changes big and small, why are some so panicked by the suggestion that it is time to reevaluate what has happened and where we ought to go from here? Of course, there are on the margins a few people who think Vatican II was a mistake and would repeal everything, legitimate and illegitimate, done in its name. But they are just that, on the margins and certain to stay there. They in no way represent what is meant by a reform of the reform.

So many good things have been done since the Council, and so much that is doubtful or wrongheaded. The reform of the reform is nothing more than a proposal that we try to sort them out. Bishop Trautman is right in sensing a widespread and growing uneasiness with the direction of liturgical change. But his strident depiction of those who disagree as enemies of the Council and persecutors of the "best and brightest" can lead only to sterile polarization, and a deepening of the suspicion that the liturgical establishment holds in contempt both the tradition of the Church and the sensibilities of the faithful who, despite all, persist in their faithfulness.

Chapter 6

1. See David Tracy, *The Analogical Imagination* (reprint, Herder & Herder, 1998).

2. I am indebted to the theologian Robert Jenson for the formulation "The gospel of Jesus Christ is the story of the world." He has developed this understanding with systematic care in his many writings.

3. Michael Polanyi, *Personal Knowledge: Towards a Post-Critical Philosophy* (University of Chicago Press, 1974).

4. For a succinct statement of what is meant by development, see Avery Dulles, "True and False Development," *First Things*, no. 135 (August/September 2003): 14–19.

5. John Lukacs, *Remembered Past* (Intercollegiate Studies Institute, 2005), 121.

6. On Clement XIII and the Jesuits, see Heinz-Joachim Fischer, *Pope Benedict XVI* (Crossroad Publishing Company, 2005), 41.

Chapter 7

1. Harold Rosenberg, "The Tradition of the New," *Commentary* (June 1959).

2. Paul Shaughnessy, "Are the Jesuits Catholic?" A review of "Passionate Uncertainty," *The Weekly Standard* 007, no. 37 (June 3, 2002).

3. Peter J. Boyer, "A Hard Faith," *New Yorker* (May 16, 2005).

4. See the author's "Mr. Wills for the Prosecution," *First Things* (November 2002).

Index

Index

Calvin, John, 105, 226
Casel, Odo, 117
Castrillion Hoyos, Dario, 209
Catherine, Saint, 74
Chaput, Archbishop Charles, 191
Charles, Prince, 206
Chelsea XII, 188
Chesterton, G. K., 10, 106, 163,
    199–202, 242
Chiesa, Giocomo della. *See* Benedict
    XV
Chirac, Jacques, 227
Churchill, Winston, 161–162, 234
Clement XIII, 169
Congar, Yves, 89–90, 160, 194
Constantine, 74
Cornwell, John, 225
Crosby, Bing, 141
Curran, Father Charles, 100–101
Cyprian, Saint, 36

Dalin, David, 225
Daneels, Godfried Cardinal, 216–217
Daniélou, Jean, 194
Darrow, Clarence, 7
Darwin, Charles, 7
Davis, Father Charles, 193
Day, Dorothy, 243
Day, Thomas, 111, 113
Decter, Midge, 177
Dewart, Leslie, 194
Dias, Ivan, 209, 214, 218
Dinoia, Archie, 122–134, 161
Diognetus, 150–151
Duffy, Eamon, 119, 222
Dulles, Avery Cardinal, 11–12, 14,
    32, 113, 235

Eliot, T. S., 51
Elizabeth I, 56

Emerson, Ralph Waldo, 89

Forster, E. M., 177
Fox, Matthew, 99, 100, 102

George, Francis Cardinal, 210,
    218–219
Gilbert, W. S., 177
Glendon, Mary Ann, 219
Greeley, Father Andrew, 217
Guardini, Romano, 117
Gumpel, Father Peter, 219, 221, 225

Hart, David, 246
Heiler, Friedrich, 117
Hellriegel, Monsignor Martin, 117
Henry VIII, 94
Heschel, Rabbi Abraham Joshua,
    207–208
Hitler, Adolf, 37, 210
Hummes, Claudio, 209, 214

Ignatius of Loyola, Saint, 13
Irenaeus, 74, 151
Isaiah, 157

James, William, 89
Jerome, Saint, 144
John, Saint, 239
John (apostle), 78
John II, 222
John Paul II (John Paul the Great;
    Karol Wojtyla), 1–3, 32, 69, 73,
    74, 91, 96, 98, 99, 129, 143,
    144–145, 146–147, 148–149,
    150, 154, 155, 156–157, 160,
    173, 178, 181, 186, 191, 192,
    194, 196, 197, 198, 203–206,
    207–208, 209, 210, 211, 213,
    214, 215–216, 217, 218, 219,

258

220, 221–222, 223, 225–226,
229, 231, 234, 235–236,
237–238, 240, 241, 242, 244,
245–246, 247
John Paul the Great. *See* John Paul II
John the Evangelist, Saint, 32
John XXIII, 179, 189, 203, 214
Jones, Jennifer, 141
Joyce, James, 134–135
Jude, 163
Jungmann, Josef, 117

Keiller, Garrison, 34, 35
Kennedy, John F., 121, 141, 180
Kierkegaard, Soren, 53, 153
King, Martin Luther, Jr., 155
Knippers, Diane, 228, 229
Knox, Ronald, 52
Koenker, Ernest, 116
Koppel, Ted, 236–237
Kretzman, O. P., 38
Küng, Father Hans, 99–100, 194,
195, 234

Law, Bernard Cardinal, 212
Lefebvre, Archbishop Marcel,
92–93, 133, 178, 179
Leo IX, 238
Lewis, C. S., 143
Lickona, Matthew, 243
Lonergan, Bernard, 194
Lubac, Henri de, 194
Lukacs, John, 166–167
Lustiger, Cardinal, 223
Luther, Martin, 38, 40, 44, 46, 48,
50, 54, 63, 75, 101, 105, 153

MacIntyre, Alasdair, 145–146, 148,
149
Maritain, Jacques, 194

Martini, Carlo Maria, 217, 223
Marx, Karl, 158
Mary Magdalene, 101
Mary (mother of Jesus), 68, 77–78,
101, 106, 108
McBrien, Father Richard, 181,
183–184, 190–191, 228–229
McCarthy, Joe, 7
McCarthy, Mary, 158
Mencken, H. L., 6, 7
Menendez, Pedro, 35
Merton, Thomas, 112, 243
Michel, Virgil, 117
Michelangelo, 73
Miller, Patrick, 43
Milton, John, 165
Montini, Giovanni Battista. *See* Paul
VI
Murphy, Father Francis X. *See*
Rynne, Xavier
Murray, Father John Courtney, 193,
194

Neuhaus (father), 34, 40, 41, 43, 46,
47–49
Newman, John Henry, 13, 25, 33,
56–57, 62, 65, 75, 78, 79, 98,
161, 163, 245
Nietzsche, Friedrich, 3
Noll, Mark, 34
Novak, Michael, 219

O'Brien, Archbishop Edward, 196
O'Connor, Edwin, 243
O'Connor, Flannery, 29, 158, 243
O'Connor, John Cardinal, 11,
31–32, 67, 244–245

Parsch, Pius, 117
Paul, Saint, 18, 24–25, 37, 44, 73–74,